M000166898

SECRET
TUSCANY

Jacopo Mauro and Roberto Di Ferdinando

JONGLEZ PUBLISHING

unusual guide

Secret *Tuscany* is the result of an observation: the guidebooks available to the inhabitants of Tuscany and frequent visitors to the region all seem to describe the same familiar places. There is nothing or very little in them that would surprise anyone who already knows the region fairly well.

This guide is aimed at such readers, although we hope it will also please the occasional visitor seeking to depart from the beaten tourist paths.

Comments on the guide or information on places we may not have mentioned are more than welcome and will help us to improve future editions.
Don't hesitate to contact us:
Jonglez publishing, 25 rue du Maréchal Foch,
   78000 Versailles, France.
   e-mail: info@jonglezpublishing.com

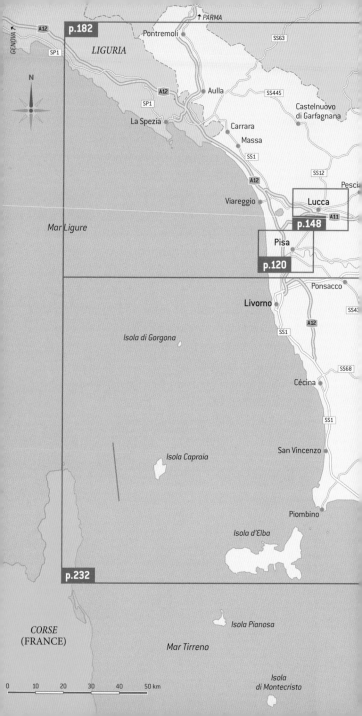

p.182

GENOVA

A12

SP1

LIGURIA

↑ PARMA

Pontremoli

SS63

N

A12

SP1

Aulla

SS445

Castelnuovo
di Garfagnana

La Spezia

Carrara

Massa

SS1

SS12

A12

Pescia

Mar Ligure

Viareggio

Lucca

p.148

A11

Pisa

p.120

Ponsacco

Livorno

SS43

A12

SS1

Isola di Gorgona

SS68

Cécina

SS1

Isola Capraia

San Vincenzo

Piombino

p.232

Isola d'Elba

CORSE
(FRANCE)

Isola Pianosa

Mar Tirreno

Isola
di Montecristo

0   10   20   30   40   50 km

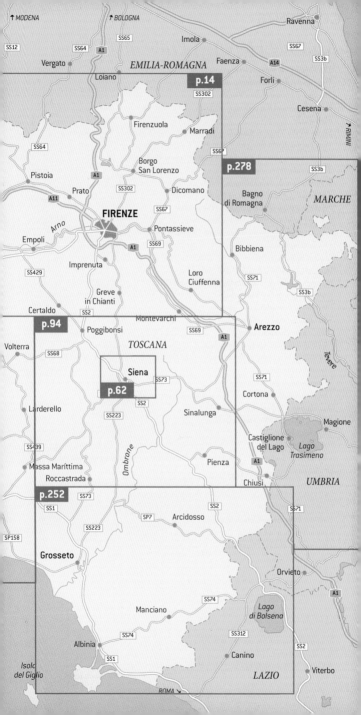

CONTENTS

Outside Florence, Prato and Pistoia

Siena

Outside Siena

CONTENTS

Pisa

Lucca

North West

CONTENTS

Livorno and surroundings

Grosseto and surroundings

Arezzo and surroundings

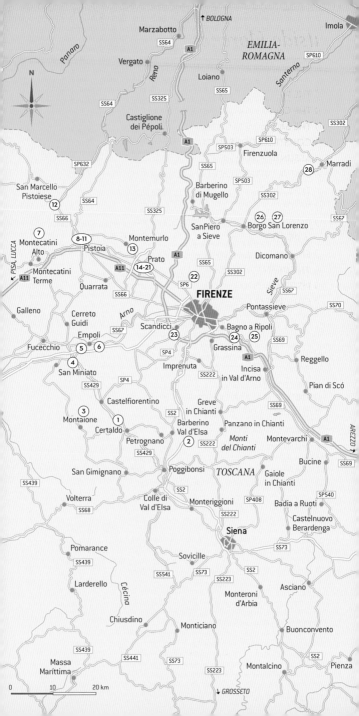

Outside Florence, Prato and Pistoia

THE PRISONS OF PALAZZO PRETORIO

A moving tale of despair etched onto prison walls

Via Boccaccio - 50052 Certaldo (FI)
Tel: 0571 66 12 19
Opening hours: in summer, daily 10.00-19.00; in winter, daily (except Monday) 10.00-16.30
Admission: 3 €, reduced: 1.50 €

Located near the top of the main street in the elegant old town of Certaldo, Palazzo Pretorio contains courtrooms, torture rooms, and cells – each of which has fascinating details. In the audience chamber, the wall bears the magistrate's motto: "Listen to the opposing side…without believing too much." To the side of this room, a large holding cell has walls covered with graffiti. The words reach up to the vaulted ceiling; it is even said that the prisoners formed human pyramids so that one of their number could get up to use whatever blank space was left. The signatures on the walls include those of "Giambadia Neri, Castelfiorentino" and "Giambattista Perazini 1555." A regular of this prison, Giambadia was something of an artist. One finds mention of him in another inscription made using candle soot. "Oh, how badly things are going for you, my friend. When you have set foot inside, it no longer depends on you when you leave. Giambadia knows this, and that is why he is telling you."

The prison for male convicts is particularly appalling, with narrow windowless cells that can only be reached by crawling through a low and very narrow tunnel. One of the three extant cells can still be visited. On the walls, the graffiti from the period gives us some idea of how atrocious a prisoner's life must have been. Look, for example, at the sun scratched into the wall, each ray representing a day that the prisoner has been shut away in this dungeon. The torture chamber was linked directly with the cells, making it possible to extract confessions more efficiently.

NEARBY

The cupola of the Semifonte chapel ②

Chapel of San Michele Arcangelo
Semifonte
50021 Barberino Val d'Elsa (FI)
Opening hours: Sunday 15.30-19.30.
Free admission
Directions: Take the road from Barberino to Certaldo. The chapel is 1km beyond the village of Petrognano

The chapel of San Michele Arcangelo at Barberino Val d'Elsa is remarkable in that its cupola is a perfect model (scale 1:8) of the dome of Florence Cathedral.

The 12th century was a period of economic boom for the town of Semifonte, due largely to the settlement's location on the Via Francigena. Enclosed by more than three kilometres of walls, the town had a population of some 300 families, each engaged in various business activities. Viewing this success with a jaundiced eye, the Florentines attempted to take the town a number of times, and finally succeeded after a long, hard siege. Their animus was such that they razed the place to the ground, forbidding future reconstruction. It was not until 1594 that anything would be built here: a chapel for which Giovan Battista di Neri Capponi had obtained permission from the Grande Duke, Ferdinando I. Consecrated in 1597, the chapel and its replica cupola had a double function: acknowledging Florentine dominion, it was also a reminder that it was the Florentines who had destroyed Semifonte.

THE SACRO MONTE OF SAN VIVALDO

An amazing reconstruction of Christ's Passion

Convent of San Vivaldo
San Vivaldo
50050 Montaione (FI)

Created on the site where Vivaldo de San Gimignano* died, the San Valdo Sacro Monte recreates various places associated with the life and final Passion of Christ. The twenty or so extant chapels (in the 16th century there were a total of 34) are adorned with sculpted reliefs and frescoes that depict such scenes as the Flight into Egypt and "Noli Me Tangere" ("Do Not Touch Me," the words used by the risen Christ to Mary Magdalene). There is also a House of Herod, a House of Caiaphas the High Priest and a House of St. Anne (the Virgin's mother). The entire place has a very special atmosphere – particularly during periods of good weather, when masses and religious services are held here.

The idea for such "holy mounts" dates back to the 15th/16th century. They were created so that the faithful could, without exposing themselves to all of the hazards of a journey to the Holy Land, still make a pilgrimage that evoked the scenes of Christ's Passion. The Franciscan Friars Minor chose three locations for these "New Jerusalems:" Varallo in Lombardy, Montaione in Tuscany and Braga in Portugal.

After the Council of Trent, they also became an increasingly effective way of combating the influence of the Protestant Reform. The model

most frequently followed was that of the Varallo Sacro Monte, which had been created in about 1480. Throughout the 16th and 17th centuries, and even up to the middle of the 18th, more sacri monti were created throughout Italy – for example at Crea, Orta, Varese, Oropa, Ossuccio, Ghiffa, Domodossola and Valperga – dedicated not only to the life of Christ but also to the Virgin, the Holy Trinity, the Rosary, and the lives of the saints. Although at the beginning they followed similar basic rules, as the years went on, each would develop its own artistic and architectural characteristics.

* *Vivaldo de San Gimignano (c.1250-1320). Now beatified, Vivaldo de San Gimignano was a hermit who lived in the hollowed trunk of a chestnut tree, on the site of which it is said that the monastery dedicated to his name was later built. The truth is that there was already a church here, dedicated to an earlier Vivaldo.*

CONSTELLATIONS OF THE CATHEDRAL OF SANTA MARIA ASSUNTA E SAN GENESIO

④

Ursa Major, Ursa Minor, and the Pole Star on a cathedral façade

Prato del Duomo
56027 San Miniato (PI)

The brick façade of the cathedral of San Miniato is adorned with 32 majolica bowls of unknown origin (perhaps from Moorish Spain, perhaps from North Africa). They are, curiously enough, laid out to recreate the two constellations of Ursa Major and Ursa Minor. At the top is a white and green star that represents the Pole Star. The originals of these majolica bowls are now in the Episcopal Palace.

The ornamentation was installed at the behest of Emperor Fredrick II, who was passionately interested in astronomy and astrology. He was also responsible for the construction of the nearby fortress and the tower that bears his name; destroyed by the Germans in 1944, it was rebuilt in 1958.

The constellations are a symbolic representation of the heaven in which the earthly journey of the Christian should culminate. Similarly, the Pole Star, in the north, is the direction towards which the compass needle points, and symbolically associated with the first gesture of the Sign of the Cross, upwards, towards God the Father.

Frederic II

Fredrick II (1194-1250) was born on a special podium raised in the main square of Jesi (near Ancona); the bed on which his mother gave birth was closely guarded so that no one could claim the child was a changeling and therefore contest his right to the crown. Orphaned when very young, Frederick was already King of Sicily when he was crowned Holy Roman Emperor in 1220. This coronation came after a series of historic turnarounds, the most spectacular of which was the defeat of his rival, Otto IV, at the battle of Bouvines (France) in 1214. Various features of the emperor's biography – his relations with various popes, the crusade he undertook, his amazing number of wives and lovers (he had a veritable harem), and the number of children he sired – all these make him into a character who seems somehow to symbolise the time in which he lived, a period of both enlightenment and trepidation. Author of a manual on falconry and a champion of what might be considered modern medicine, Frederick was a skilful politician who spoke nine languages. Throughout his life he would avoid staying in Florence (then called Florentia) because he had been told that he would die in a city whose name contained the word 'flower' [fiore in Italian]. However, he met his death at a place whose name he did not know: Castel Fiorentino. There are numerous traces of Frederick II in Italy, most notably the Castel del Monte which he had built at Andria in Puglia – this now appears on the 1 eurocent coin.

STATUE OF THE VIRGIN IN THE CLOISTER OF THE COLLEGIATE CHURCH OF SANT'ANDREA

A Catholic sculpture paid for by a ghetto Jew...

Museum of the Collegiate Church of Sant'Andrea
3, Piazzetta della Propositura
50053 Empoli (FI)
Tel: 0571 76284
E-mail: cultura@comune.empoli.fi.it
Opening hours: 9.00-12.00 and 16.00-19.00. Closed Monday
Admission: 3 €, reduced: 1.5 €

The glazed terracotta statue of the Virgin and Child in the cloister of the Collegiate Church of Sant'Andrea is by the Della Robbia school. Curiously enough, it was paid for by a Jewish resident of the town's ghetto.

In 1518, whilst the Corpus Christi procession was passing by his house, the banker Zaccaria d'Isacco could not resist – perhaps because of the tension caused by the recent imposed baptism of a Jewish infant –

« Photograph: Museo della Collegiata di Sant'Andrea »

making derogatory comments when the baldaquin with the monstrance (a receptacle for the Host) came to a halt beneath his windows. Tried in Florence – to avoid public indignation resulting in violence – the banker was sentenced to pay for a statue of the Virgin and Child. Originally set into the façade of the Palazzo Pretorio, the statue was moved to its present location during the period of Napoleonic rule: it was considered to be too crude a reminder of religious intolerance. The circumstances which resulted in the removal of the infant's head are unknown.

NEARBY

Wooden wings of a flying ass
Cloister Museum of the Collegiate Church of Sant'Andrea
3, Piazzetta della Propositura - 50053 Empoli (FI)

In the same cloister as the statue of the Virgin (see above) is a curious pair of wood wings (complete with pulleys) suspended from the ceiling. These were the wings for the ass which "flew" each year from the top of the bell tower down to Piazza Farinata degli Uberti (also known as Piazza dei Leoni) during the evening which ended the Corpus Domini celebrations. The tradition dated back to 1397, when the forces of the city of Empoli took the castle of San Miniato, which had been considered impregnable. The besieging forces had hit upon the ruse of strapping lamps to a thousand goats which they then drove up towards the castle: believing that they were massively outnumbered, the defenders surrendered and opened their gates to avoid being put to the sword. The Captain of the castle, a certain Silvera, had previously boasted that he would surrender when asses could fly – and thus the tradition of the "flying ass" was a mocking reference to his words. The poor animal concerned was strapped into a winged harness (as you can see at the museum) which ran on two pulleys along a rope. From the top of the bell tower, the creature was then released to travel the length of the cable and smash against one of the columns in the piazza. The custom was finally banned in 1860 – not only because of its cruelty but also because it mocked Empoli's ancient rival of San Miniato. In 1981 an attempt was made to revive the custom using a model of an ass; but due to its cost, this revival lasted only a few years.

PASSION CROSS IN THE MONASTERY OF SANTA MARIA A RIPA

A depiction of the instruments of Christ's Passion

36, Via Porta di Borgo
51016 Montecatini Alto (PT)
Tel: 0572 91 15 88
Park in the small area in front of the monastery. The Cross is to one side of the
steps that lead to the church.

This fine example of a Passion Cross at Santa Maria a Ripa is noteworthy not only for its size but also for its detailed reproductions of the implements used by Christ's tormenters (most of these are in wood).

From the top to the bottom of the Cross, one finds a total of thirty or so such objects: the panel reading 'INRI' [Jesus of Nazareth, King of the Jews], the Crown of Thorns, the hand symbolising that washed by Pontius Pilate, the Vernicle bearing the image of Christ's face (not to be confused with the Holy Shroud, see below), the sword with which Peter cut off the ear of Malchus, the lantern by whose light Malchus recognised Jesus in the Garden of Olives, the cup in which Christ's blood was collected (this would become the Holy Grail) the tunic for which the Roman soldiers cast dice (along with the dice immediately below), and the veil of the maidservant Ancilla. Right at the base of the Cross is a skull that recalls the place of Christ's crucifixion, Mount Golgotha (gulgota in Aramaic means "skull").

On the left arm of the Cross are: the rope used to heave it into place, the spear which pierced Christ's side, the pitcher containing the vinegar he was given to drink, the pincers used to draw out the nails, and the ladder used to bring his body down after the crucifixion. Located on the right arm are the column to which Christ was bound during the flagellation, the cockerel which crowed three times, the hammer which drove in the nails, the long rod with the sponge soaked in vinegar, and the whip with flails. The three nails themselves are in the places where they held Christ's hands and feet.

This already impressive list of items also includes the purse with the thirty pieces of silver which Judas accepted to betray Christ, the heart symbolising Christ's love for humankind, and the Sun recalling that there was an eclipse of three hours at Christ's death.

The vernicle

According to the apocryphal gospels (particularly that of Nicodemus), as Christ was bearing his Cross to Golgotha a woman drew off her veil to wipe his brow. The image of Christ's face would remain imprinted on the material and miraculously survive over the centuries. Later, the name of this woman would be given as Veronica, from the Latin vero (true) and the Greek icon (image), with the veil itself becoming known in English as the Vernicle. Various churches (in Rome, Milan or Jaén in Spain) claim to possess the original Vernicle. The one now displayed in St. Peter's in Rome was first described in 1137.

ENIGMATIC HEADS ON BUILDINGS IN PISTOIA ⑧

Heads up...

Palazzo Communale, Piazza del Duomo
Church of Sant'Andrea, Via Sant'Andrea
Corner of Via Sant'Andrea and Via de'Rossi
Via Borgostrada (first wall on the left upon leaving Piazza dello Spirito Santo)

When visiting Pistoia, you would do well to glance upwards now and again: numerous walls and buildings are adorned with sculpted heads whose meaning is not always clear.

The most spectacular – and best known – of these heads is to be found on the façade of the Palazzo Communale. It is surmounted by an arm brandishing a weapon; the sharp-eyed will also make out a bunch of keys hanging around the arm itself. Some have claimed that the head depicts King Musetto of Majorca, who was defeated by the Pistoia-born Grandone de' Ghisilieri when the Pisan fleet conquered the Balearic Islands in 1115. However, a more likely suspect would be Filippo Tedici, who treacherously seized power in 1325 with the backing of the town of Lucca. Having been overthrown and driven out of Pistoia, he would later try to incite a popular uprising against the occupying forces of Guelph-controlled Florence. But recognised by some peasants at the Castruccio bridge which crossed the river Lima near Popiglio (see Castruccio Castracani in the section on Lucca, page 185), Tedici was killed and his head was then borne in triumph to Pistoia on a pike. The city's Council of Elders would decide that marble effigies of the traitor should be carved and placed at various points in Pistoia (ruling of 7 September 1336) as a warning to other traitors.

As for the keys, they open the doors to the city gaols. They were added in 1399, when those still languishing in prison as a result of intestine strife were finally released thanks to the intercession of the bishop, Andrea Franchi, and the payment of a ransom collected during a day of penitence.

Effigies of the head of Filippo Tedici are to be found in three other places: at the corner of Via Sant'Andrea and Via de' Rossi, on a column to the right of the main doorway to the church of Sant'Andrea and at the beginning of Via Borgostrada as it leads out of Piazza dello Spirito Santo. The face embedded in the Sant'Andrea column in fact looks more porcine than human. It is said that the city gravediggers used to show their contempt for the traitor by extinguishing their torches against the effigy.

THE DEATH OF GERMANICUS BY NICOLAS POUSSIN

When Poussin copied his own paintings...

Corner Room C
Museo Clemente Rospigliosi
9, Via Ripa del Sale - 51100 Pistoia (PT)
Tel: 0573 28 740
Opening hours: Tuesday to Saturday 10.00-13.00 and 18.00-19.00

Connoisseurs visiting the Museo Rospigliosi in Pistoia will undoubtedly come to a halt before the painting entitled *The Death of Germanicus*. An extremely faithful copy of the original work by Nicolas Poussin, this is remarkable in that it was painted by Poussin himself.

Seeking to study Italian painting that he admired so much, Poussin set out for Rome, where he hoped to perfect his own art. However, health problems meant that his first two attempts to get there were unsuccessful. During his first journey, he intended to stop in Florence, but due to sickness he had to spend some time convalescing in Pistoia, where he lodged with the Puccini family. To thank his hosts, he painted this copy of *The Death of Germanicus*, a work he had previously carried out for Cardinal Barberini.

As Félibien notes, Poussin "preferred to be the copyist of his own works, rather than entrusting the task to someone else." The original painting would remain in the Barberini collection until 1958, when it was acquired by the Minneapolis Institute of Arts.

Mystic marriage of the bishop and the abbess

Up to the middle of the 16th century, the appointment of a new bishop in Pistoia was marked by the very unusual ceremony of a "mystic marriage."

The future bishop passed the night before his investiture outside the city, on the road from Pistoia to Lucca. Garbed in his ceremonial vestments, he rode into the town the next day on a white horse, accompanied by various local notables; from the gate on the Pistoia-Lucca road, he then processed to the church of the convent of San Pietro.

Here, a ceremony of "marriage" between the bishop and the abbess of the convent was performed. After an exchange of rings, the two knelt beside a richly adorned bed set up in the centre of the church. The ceremony binding together the bishop and the main female figure of authority in Pistoia was seen as marking the union of civil and religious power.

One can well imagine the determination with which the Counter Reformation set about abolishing the sexual symbolism of the bed and the exchange of rings... and eventually the entire ceremony itself. However, the event did survive in the work of a Danish artist, Kristian Zahrtmann, an indefatigable explorer of all things Italian. When he heard of this curious – but by then extinct – custom, Zahrtmann made it the subject of a spectacular work, his *The Mystic Marriage of Pistoia* (The marriage between the Bishop and Abbess of Pistoia celebrated before the church of san Pietro in the year 1500).

Measuring 1.23 metre by 1.46, the work was exhibited for the first time in Copenhagen in 1894; it is now to be found in the Museum of the Island of Bornholm in Denmark. A fascinating book entitled *Kristian Zahrtmann e il Matrimonio Mistico di Pistoia* is on sale for 18 euros at the Pistoia city museum (unfortunately it is only available in Italian).

Along with numerous illustrations of Zahrtmann's work, the book contains a fine reproduction of the painting.

PISTOIA MUSEUM OF SURGICAL IMPLEMENTS

An extraordinary anatomy theatre

Ospedale del Ceppo
1, Piazza Giovanni XXIII
51100 Pistoia (PT)
Free admission, but visits by appointment only
Tel: 0573 35 20 40

S till a functioning hospital, the Ospedale del Ceppo contains a Museum of Surgical Implements that is a veritable gem.

The high point of the visit is the extraordinary 17th century anatomy theatre. This has recently been restored, complete with original furnishings which give one a vivid idea of what the place must have once been like. The anteroom is dominated by a simple white marble slab, where the cadaver was laid out before the lesson began. A curious hinged contraption in wood made it possible to hold the limbs in place ready for study. In the second room are the narrow benches of the amphitheatre. The place could seat around forty students, all gazing down at the second marble slab where the anatomical dissection actually took place. The room's walls are decorated with painted grotesques that are strangely out of keeping with the purpose of the theatre itself.

The museum proper begins with a room containing exhibits of dozens of surgical implements dating from the 18th and 19th century. Used by obstetricians, urologists, and orthopaedists, some of these tools were manufactured outside Italy (in France and England) but most were produced in Pistoia itself, a city still renowned for its skill in this field. The exhibits include a pair of the famous forceps invented at the beginning of the eighteenth century by Peter Chamberlen, a Frenchman with an Anglicised name. In fact, he long kept the design of a secret so as to enjoy a very profitable exclusivity over his invention... And don't miss the amazing obstetric "machine," which enabled students to perform simulated deliveries. Damaged during the bombing raids of the Second World War, this contraption has unfortunately lost the accessories that went with it: a false placenta made out of fabric, a toy baby, and a dead foetus.

The hospital owes its curious name (*del ceppo* means "of the stump") to that fact that the stump of a chestnut tree was used to collect donations towards the cost of the original building.

GIUSEPPE GHERARDESCHI
INTERNATIONAL ORGAN ACADEMY

Unusual concerts combining two organs

Church of the Holy Ghost or Church of St. Ignatius of Loyola
Piazza dello Spirito Santo, 8 - 51100 Pistoia (PT)
Open: Daily 8:30am—12:30pm and 4pm—6pm
Tel: 057-328-787 or 335-682-5318
Email: info@accademiagherardeschi.it
www.accademiagherardeschi.it

While the Province of Pistoia does not possess a record number of church organs, or have a particular tradition of them, music courses have been available there since 1975. The academy's international involvement has provided resources for restoring and preserving some very valuable instruments, such as a 1793 Luigi Benedetto Tronci organ in Pistoia Cathedral. In particular it has allowed the conservation of a 1664 Wilhelm Hermans instrument housed in the Church of the Holy Ghost. There are two organs in this church positioned opposite one another. The second dates from 2007 and was added specifically so that concerts could be performed using this unusual configuration.

The academy also has several early baroque musical instruments, including a 1731 spinet in perfect working order. It once belonged to Ludovico Giustini from Pistoia, the first musician to publish sonatas for the pianoforte, which had been newly invented at that time.

All these instruments can be seen upon request. And if any musician is able to play them, they are completely free to do so irrespective of their technical ability. Baroque music weekends are also organised by the academy, as well, of course, as organ concerts. The program for these events can be found on the academy's website. Entry to these evenings is always free.

The Empress of Japan in Pistoia

Since the town of Pistoia became a special centre for the church organ in 1985, it has been twinned with the Japanese town of Shirakawa. An enthusiast of these instruments, the Empress of Japan visited Pistoia in 1993.

THE MADONNINA ICE HOUSE ⑫
Italy's old fridge

Via Modenese, SR (Regional Road) 66, Le Piastre (Province of Pistoia)
Open: Guided tours in July and August on Saturdays and Sundays; and on the 15th August at 4:30pm and 5:45pm; or by prior booking. There is unlimited access to the path from which exterior views of the ice house are available
Entry fee: Guided tours are 2€ per person on the days shown above. The charge is negotiable at other times
Tel: 057-397-461 - Email: ecomuseum@provincia.pistoia.it - www.ecomuseopt.it

Halfway up the road climbing from Pistoia into the Apennines is the small village of Le Piastre. The road was originally conceived by Grand Duke Leopold and completed in 1748. Le Piastre is in an area known as the Cold Valley, and not without just cause. Because of its location, temperatures here are lower than elsewhere in the vicinity. This natural characteristic has been exploited from the early part of the 18th century to produce 'natural ice'. In reality that name did not become widespread until chemical ways of lowering temperatures were introduced. That said, the ice industry grew in importance, the market extending further afield in Italy as access roads, and later railways, improved. In its heyday, ice from this valley was sent as far as Rome in special metal-walled wagons. The industry continued up to the 1940s. A fine local example of such ice houses lives on today — the Madonnina. It can be seen from the outside just by walking along the path that leads to it. Or it can be visited on request, accompanied by a guide (see details above). Its structure is like a tree trunk in shape and designed to take full advantage of the natural thermal inertia of ice. The layers of ice were separated by chestnut leaves and stored here until removed from the building to be sold in the towns below. Removal was by way of three openings at various levels depending on the mode of transport used. To fill

an ice house like the Madonnina, it took three *lagate* (layers of ice), which meant that the artificial pool above the valley had to freeze over three times and the ice had to be harvested three times in order to fill the ice house. If you have visited La Madonnina and would like to acquire a better understanding of how the ice was worked, there is an educational hub where original documents passed down through the families of the "*ghiacciatori*" can be seen. Access to it is by request using the phone number or email address shown at the top of this page.

How was ice obtained in the Cold Valley?

The first step was to divert the flow of a local river into small hollows where artificial ponds could be formed. This had to be done in such a way that there remained a constant flow of water underneath to prevent the pond from freezing through to the bottom. If it froze completely, it would have been difficult to extract the sheets of ice. The inflow channel therefore had to be prevented from freezing up. Once the layer of ice had formed on top of the pond, the "pond chief" broke the surface using his *palamina*, a special pointed shovel. Thus "rafts" of ice were formed, akin to mini icebergs, and these were hoisted up with the aid of grappling hooks into the ice house, where another employee known as the *accomodino* moved the sheets into place.

MUSEUM OF VINTAGE AMBULANCES (AND HEARSES)

Vintage ambulances, with a friar as your guide

32, Piazza Leonardo da Vinci - 59013 Montemurlo (PO)
Tel: 339 46 23 627
Visits by appointment only
For opening hours see: www.volontari.org

Set up by the Confraternity of Montemurlo – itself a subsidiary branch of the *Venerabile Arciconfraternità della Misericordia di Prato* (see below) - this ambulance museum is an astonishing place. Located within the industrial zone of Montemurlo, it was opened in October 2006 and has more than 50 ambulances and 10 hearses, all in perfect condition. The earliest exhibits date back to when the sick were carried on foot by stretcher bearers. Thereafter are examples of cars adapted by local body shops to serve as ambulances; this was in the days before such vehicles were purpose-built. Each ambulance is accompanied by the relevant technical details. But what brings this museum to life is the commentary provided by the friar from the confraternity 'brother' who accompanies you and knows anecdotes relating to each ambulance.

The 1943 Willys MB Jeep, for example, arrived in Italy with American troops during the Second World War. After the war it was bought by Father Aldo Fazzini, parish priest of Schignano, and was converted into an ambulance by a body shop in Prato. It would perform sterling service right up to the day that the group bought it for the museum and then restored it before putting it on display. When Father Fazzini came to visit the museum and saw the old ambulance, his eyes lit up. "That's her!" he said, without further comment.

Confraternita della Misericordia

These confraternities were founded in the 13th century to assist pilgrims and provide them with lodging. Catholic in origin, they would adapt over the centuries to met the needs of changing events (epidemics, famine, war) and societies, concerning themselves not only with the transport of the sick and wounded but also with the collectionof those who died penniless in the street and even with the collection of funds to provide needy young women with dowries. The brothers of the confraternity wore a long ankle-length robe, which during the plague of 1630 became black in colour (in order to hide the stains left by the discharge from purulent sores). They also wore a hood with two eyeholes, which was intended to guarantee that their charitable work remained anonymous. Their robes, complete with a rope that serves as a belt, have remained unchanged to the present day, when they are only worn for formal processions.

Today, the various *Confraternita della Misericordia* are the backbone of Italy's ambulance services.

MUSEUM OF DEPORTATION

Tuscany's place of remembrance for the world

Via di Cantagallo, 250
59100 Prato (PO) (in the hamlet of Figline)
Open: Mon—Fri 9:30am—12:30pm; Also Monday, Thursday, Saturday and Sunday 3pm—6pm (summer opening hours from June to September 4pm7pm). Closed for three weeks in August.
(Special opening for organised visits or school groups by prior arrangement)
Free entry — donations accepted for guided visits
Tel: 057-446-1655 or 057-447-0728
Email: info@museodelladeportazione.it
www.museodelladeportazione.it

The Museum of Deportation in Prato is the only one of its kind in Italy. It was opened in 2002 by the city council driven by the determination and commitment of a number of Prato residents who survived deportation to Nazi concentration camps during the Second World War. Of a total of 152 deportees, 133 were sent to Mauthausen and Ebensee camps in Austria. Only 18 survived this horror. In the 1970s some found the courage to return to the place of their suffering, the tunnels of Ebensee, where thousands of their companions in misery had died. There, the Nazis had forced them into hard labour in most inhuman conditions.

When the allied troops arrived, the SS attempted to hide as much evidence of their crimes as possible, but in fact, this had the opposite effect — it preserved almost everything just as it had been. Various objects, such as tools and other evidence of the brutal daily life in the camp, were found. Many of the original items retrieved from the Ebensee tunnels are now on display in the museum. They provide a symbolic and painful reconstruction of the world of the concentration camp. The visit is brought to life with the help of audio-visual material describing life and death in the camps through the voices of survivors.

School groups from all over Italy come to visit the museum and its resource centre. It is significant to note that the catalogue has even been translated into Chinese, helping to ensure that the memory of these horrors is kept alive in the consciousness of future generations.

NEARBY
The tabernacle of Sant'Anna

In the same village there is a small roadside votive chapel: the tabernacle of Sant'Anna. It was created by Agnolo Gaddi, a painter of the Florentine school of Giotto (second half of the 14th century) and is well worth making a detour for. It is unusual by virtue of its exceptional size (18 square metres) and particularly its rare *mettarza* representation, whereby behind the Virgin and Child, and larger than them, appears Saint Anne, serving as a reminder of her importance as the mother of the mother of Christ.

The tabernacle is situated next to the parish church of San Pietro (*Pieve di San Pietro*) on the ancient medieval route to Bologna — also worth a visit.

THE SANPAO BUDDHIST TEMPLE

A Buddhist temple in a disused factory

Piazza della Gualchierina, 19
59100 Prato (PO)
Open: Daily 6am—5pm with collective prayers from 6:30am—7:30am
Tel: 057-440-0152

Since its inception in September 2009, the Sanpao Buddhist temple has been a central hub for the many Chinese people who live and work in Prato (see box below), as well as for members of other ethnic minorities such as Indian and Pakistani residents. Located on a small square close to the historic centre, the simple premises it occupies were once a *gualchiera*, or cloth-beating factory, long since closed down and abandoned, just like its neighbour.

On entering this building, so plainly intended for industrial use, elderly Chinese volunteers make you welcome. There is little Italian spoken, but this does not mean you will feel any less welcome as everybody here makes an effort to communicate with each other. After walking to the end of the first corridor, visitors will be greeted by several large statues of the Buddha and his guardians. Three rooms are divided up by some very distinctive statues, altars, incense, red lanterns, drums, prayer tables and prie-dieus. After just a short walk, visitors feel as if they have stepped into the Orient.

This temple is not simply a place of worship. It also acts as a headquarters for the Buddhist Association and the Chinese community in Italy. It is involved in organising cultural initiatives, such as the celebration of the Chinese New Year, and assists with providing funds for such causes as the purchase of ambulances for the region's Red Cross and the provision of assistance to earthquake victims. Moreover, it serves as a place where Italian citizens can meet the Chinese community, which has been settled in Prato for over ten years and continues to flourish.

The Chinese community in Prato: about 20 per cent of the population

Nowadays, approximately 20 per cent of the population of Prato is of Chinese origin. Many oriental residents of Prato first arrived at least 20 years ago to settle in this Tuscan manufacturing town and work in the textile sector. For the most part they have settled in industrial areas, particularly along the Via Pistoiese, which has slowly evolved into a genuine Chinatown — you don't have to wander far from the historic centre through the Porta Pistoiese to find yourself among the smells, the wares, the fruits and vegetables, with signs, shops and locals, all of them Chinese. At first sight there is no doubt that the houses and apartment blocks are Italian, with their green shutters and cypress trees dotted here and there. But it isn't long before all these other things make you wonder if you are actually in China.

THE HISTORIC PHARMACY OF THE MONASTERY AND CONSERVATORY OF SAN NICCOLÒ DI PRATO

A magnificent historic pharmacy, a holy staircase and a folding crucifix

Piazza Niccolò Cardinale, 6 - 59100 Prato (PO)
Open: Visits lasting about two hours can be made on the first Saturday of the month at 3pm (except in July and August) or by phoning the caretaker
Tel: 0574-26103 (caretaker); 0574-433-082 (administrative office) - www.sniccolo.it

If you looked down on the centre of Prato from space, to the west of the town you would see two vast green spaces. These spaces are within the ancient town walls, but what you would be seeing is not a public park. These are actually the *orti di gosto* (vegetable gardens) of the San Niccolò Monastery, where fruit and vegetables are still grown today. In the old days they were used to produce the different medicinal plants that the magnificent pharmacy in the heart of the complex would in turn dispense. This monastery, active since at least 1328, has always been run by Dominican nuns, although it was transformed into a foundation under private law in 2006. In the past there was a girls' school at this site. It was reserved for young daughters of the nobility — the school annex is still in existence, although it has changed somewhat. Its approximately 400 pupils range in age between 18 months and 18 years and it is a private school. The staff primarily consists of former pupils and teaching takes place for the most part in rooms of monumental proportions, some with a long history. The complex shelters a number of treasures unknown to those who usually go there to study or work. Among these works are a nativity by Donatello, a painting on wood of the school of Botticelli, an unusual crucifix by Baccio da Montelupo (with folding arms to make it easier to transport), and an

imitation organ that matches the real one inside the main church. There is also a chapel in which one of the few known depictions of the town of Prato as it was in the Middle Ages has been painted. There is so much to discover that the visit lasts about two hours. Apart from the pharmacy you can also see two refectories and a bathroom, which is now used to receive pupils' parents. From one of the vegetable gardens rises a *scala santa* (holy staircase), which the faithful would climb on their knees. Nearby there is a *via crucis*, one of the earliest known; so early in fact, that some claim that praying at the Stations of the Cross was invented there.

The interior façade

Curiously, the most remarkable façade is the one to be found inside. The small square now overlooked by the church was closed in earlier times, but in 1785 the architect Valentini opted to add a 'modern' (for the age) touch to the colonnade surrounding the monastery's cloister.

THE HANDPRINT IN PRATO CATHEDRAL

The bloody trace of the hand that wished to steal the holy relic of the Virgin's girdle...

Piazza del Duomo - 59100 Prato (PO)

To the upper left of the second door in the south wall of the cathedral – that nearest the bell tower – is a curious age-old mark. Consisting of the print of a thumb and four fingers, it is said to belong to a thief who tried to steal the famous and precious relic of the Virgin's Girdle (see below). According to the story, around 1141 a certain Michele dei Dagomari, a resident of Prato, married the daughter of a priest in Jerusalem, a certain Maria, who brought this girdle as her dowry. After various vicissitudes, the man would donate the relic to the city in 1175. In 1312, Giovanni di Landetto, a canon living in Pistoia, managed to lay his hands on it. But on his way back home, he got lost in the fog and unwittingly walked in a circle back to one the Prato town gates. There, he shouted: "Open up, I have the Holy Girdle from Prato!" Captured, he had his right hand amputated and was then led off to be burnt at the stake. The angry crowd seized his severed hand and hurled it against the cathedral. It is said to have struck the wall at the above-mentioned place, leaving a bloody hand.

The Holy Girdle – The Dormition and Assumption of The Virgin

The relic of the Holy Girdle of the Virgin is preserved in a chapel to which it gives its name. The story associated with this relic dates back to St. Thomas, and is itself linked with the apocryphal episode of the Dormition of the Virgin (which figures primarily in the Gospel of St. John the Theologian). According to this tradition, the Virgin did not actually die but rather "fell asleep." She rendered her soul to God in the presence of all the other Apostles with the exception of St. Thomas. He arrived late and, refusing to believe in her Assumption, opened her tomb, where he found nothing but lilies and roses. Thomas then raised his head heavenwards, where he saw the Virgin in glory. Untying her girdle, she handed it to him as a gift, and as proof that she had ascended to Heaven "in body and soul." The tradition of the Dormition and Assumption did not become Church dogma until 1 November 1950 – when a five-year-old boy, Gilles Bouhours, is said to have passed on to Pope Pius XII a message he received from the Virgin, who appeared to him in visions. "The Holy Virgin is not dead," the boy told him. "she ascended to Heaven both body and soul." Note that there are three other relics of the Holy Girdle: at Puy-Notre-Dame in France, at Homs in Syria and at Istanbul in Turkey. St. Isidor, too, is said to have received the Virgin's girdle as proof of her Assumption into Heaven.

Assumption and Ascension

The Ascension refers to Christ's ascension to Heaven, while the Assumption refers to the raising of the Virgin. The latter term indicates a passive process: the body of the Virgin did not raise itself heavenward.

BASILICA OF SANTA MARIA DELLE CARCERI

When science works miracles...

Piazza Santa Maria delle Carceri
59100 Prato (PO)

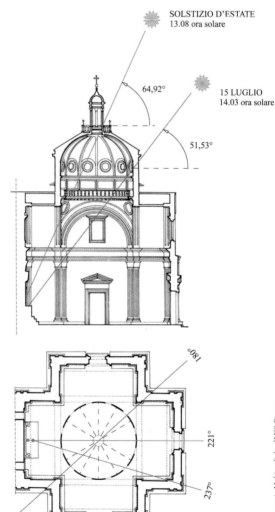

SOLSTIZIO D'ESTATE
13.08 ora solare

64,92°

15 LUGLIO
14.03 ora solare

51,53°

180°

221°

237°

©Laboratorio Multimediale - IMSS Firenze

Tradition has it that on 6 July 1484 a child saw the image of the Virgin and Child painted on the walls of the Prato prison begin to move. After the phenomenon was repeated a number of times, the basilica of Santa Maria delle Carceri ("of prisons") was built on the site. The architect Giuliano da Sangallo began work in 1485, creating a church in the form of a Greek cross. The alignment of the building was very carefully calculated so that on the anniversary of the miracle (the 15th of July according to the Gregorian calendar adopted in 1582), a ray of sunlight would fall directly onto the centre of the high altar at the precise hour of 15.19 (14.03 solar time). Furthermore, the axis of the building was so calculated that on the day of the summer solstice (21 June) the azimuth of the sun would correspond with the structure's angle of alignment (221°) and a ray of light falling down through the cupola would illuminate the revered image of the Virgin....

The intention was not so much to create belief in a new miracle as to preserve the original miracle of 1484 by reproducing it each year. The sanctuary has continued to be a place of devotion and still attracts large numbers of the faithful on these two special days.

NEARBY
Italy's largest meteor ⑳

Museum of Planetary Sciences
20/H, Via Galcianese - 59100 Prato (PO)
Tel: 0574 44 771
Email: info@mspo.it. www.mspo.it
Opening hours: from September to May, Tuesday to Sunday 8.30-13.30 and 15.00-17.00; June to August, Tuesday to Friday 9.00-13.00 and 17.00-23.00, Saturday and Sunday 9.00-13.00 and 16.00-20.00.
Admission: 5 €, reduced: 2.50 €

Opened in March 2005, the new Museum of Planetary Sciences in Prato contains various amazing meteorites, including the largest one in Italy. Known as the Nantan Meteorite, it weighs 272 kg – and one is even allowed to touch it! It is a rare example of a ferrous meteorite and fell near the Chinese village of Nantan in 1516, being discovered there by local peasants in 1958. Its composition is 92% iron and 7% nickel. Meteorites are in fact classified according to the weight they have while still in space, before falling into the Earth's atmosphere: if they weigh less than 50kg they are called "meteoroids", above that weight they are known as "asteroids."

PALAZZO DATINI FRESCOES

The world of a medieval merchant revealed

Palazzo Datini
Via Ser Lapo Mazzei, 43
59100 Prato (PO)
Open: Mon—Fri 9am—12:30pm and 3pm—6pm; Saturday 9am—12:30pm
Free entry
Tel: 057-421-391
Email: casapiadeiceppi@alice.it
www.museocasadatini.it

Francesco Datini's house is well known to the people of Prato, but not many of them are aware of some of the fascinating things it contains. Typically, the rooms of this fine dwelling house, completed in 1354, provide some interesting historic insight into the master of the house, his wife, their work and how they lived in Prato at the end of the 14th century.

The rooms have retained their original pink mortar tiling and are richly adorned with frescoes; one depicting Saint Christopher beside the main door is of special importance because it protects against the *malamorte* (sudden death without the opportunity to seek redemption).

The frescoes that embellish the room used for receiving clients and guests were designed to reproduce the interior of a garden that was once in front of the building. The paintings of the garden were enhanced by the addition of some animals, including an angora cat and swans, but in reality the presence of these in Prato was fairly improbable. Maybe this was intended to make the viewer look closely to find the treasures hidden in the decoration. Or perhaps these exotic touches were intended to show that it was possible to acquire in this house things that were not yet available in the rest of the town. It was this merchant's singular vision of the world that was the secret of his success, as is demonstrated by the archives that he has handed down to us (see below).

The Datini collection: lists, instructions and economic accounts of a multinational of 650 years ago

The Datini collection constitutes the most important medieval commercial archive in the world, with about 150,000 documents, including accounting ledgers, stocktaking, bills of exchange, economic accounts (double entry), orders and invoices, and some private correspondence. Actually, Datini owned and ran businesses in what is now Italy and Spain. He bought and sold all over Europe and North Africa, although he personally never left Tuscany. To achieve this he used an excellent network of associates who never failed to keep him abreast of everything that was happening — and with some detail! Facts about prices, exchanges, investments (good or bad), and collections of samples from international trading activity going back some 650 years are revealed to us. Then there are the concerns of the husband and wife and their associates. For example, we learn that Margherita wanted at all costs to know who her husband Francesco "was sleeping with" when he was staying alone in Florence or Pisa...

All these documents can be consulted at the location or freely online by visiting www.datini.archiviodistato.prato.it

LA LISCA

A whalebone, proving beyond doubt the existence of this marine monster

50055 Lastra a Signa
Autostrada 67, linking Empoli with Lastra a Signa, at the 65,300 km turn-off

The commune of Lastra a Signa includes the hamlet of La Lisca (fishbone), a curious name evocative of the marine world, from which it does in fact originate. This small community of a few houses overlooks Autostrada 67, which links Empoli with Lastra a Signa at the 65,300 km turn-off, along the banks of the Arno. In the past this spot was not only an important stopover for goods coming in from the coast, but a boarding point for the boats that ferried passengers and merchandise from one bank to the other. This ancient trade is also reflected in the name of the nearby locality of Porto di Mezzo (Middle Harbour).

In ancient times the sea came up this far, and excavations in the surrounding fields have turned up a huge bone, probably from a prehistoric whale, which the locals aptly called "La Lisca". This bone was set under the roof of a house then used as a tavern, which gave its name to this small group of houses until it came to be known as Porto di Sotto (Port Below). A plaque still visible on the house frontage tells the story of this bone, referring to a passage from *Travels in Tuscany, to observe its natural productions and ancient monuments*, by the Florentine physician and naturalist Giovanni Targioni Tozzetti (1712-1783).

The whalebone known as "La Lisca" is not the only example of the remains of huge animals displayed on the façades of Tuscan houses and churches. There are historical accounts of the remains of a beached whale found at Versilia in 1495, which was hung in the portico of the church of Santa Maria dei Servi in Lucca. Similarly, in 1549, the skeleton of a large fish that floundered near Livorno was on show for several months in Florence under the Loggia dell'Orcagna, not to mention the whale's jawbone attached to the front of the Medici Villa of Cafaggiolo in Mugello, later moved to the entrance of a townhouse.

These skeletons of gigantic animals were once regularly on public display, where they were taken for the remains of monsters from the Holy Scriptures. In this way, they served as a warning to the people that they should respect the prevailing rules and moral standards: otherwise these monsters would obviously be called upon to inflict a well-deserved punishment.

THE ARBITRARY FOUNTAIN

A work of art with a will of its own...

Parco di Poggio Valicaia, 6a, Via della Poggiona, 50018 Scandicci (FI)
www.comune.scandicci.fi.it/poggio_valicaia/index.htm
Information: Ufficio parchi e qualità della vita urbana
Tel: 055 75 91 247
E-mail: parchieverde@comune.scandicci.fi.it
Opening hours: from November to February, Saturday and Sunday 9.00-16.30;
March and October, Wednesday to Sunday 9.00-18.00; April, Wednesday to
Sunday 9.00-20.00; May and September, Tuesday to Sunday 9.00-20.00; and
June to August, Tuesday to Sunday 8.30-20.00

About six metres high and made of iron and steel, the Arbitrary Fountain is the work of Gilberto Zorio (see below). At the top is a star-shaped container that collects rainwater and dew. When the liquid is at a certain level, the water is automatically ejected via a siphon.

There is no telling when this might happen, so visitors can suddenly find themselves being doused with water. The creator's intention was to remind people that the laws of nature may be unpredictable and beyond human control.

The park itself is a haven of peace for the people of Florence, with various walks laid out to incorporate other works of art that are perfectly in keeping with the natural setting.

Gilberto Zorio

Gilberto Zorio was born in 1944 in Adorno Micca (Biella). An inhabitant of Turin, he was one of the protagonists of the 1960s revolutionary movement "Arte Povera", the "attitude" of which was to oppose the cultural industry and consumer society using a guerilla strategy. The originality of his work lies in the fact that it is generally in action. One of his most spectacular pieces is called Torcia: flaming torches fall on the work, destroying it.

Origins of the Chianti Black Rooster

The *Gallo Nero* (Black Rooster) is the emblem of Chianti: the consortium of wine producers known as Chianti Classico has even adopted it as its logo. The choice of the rooster goes back a long way: the image of the black bird on a golden background already featured in the coat-of-arms of the Chianti League, a kind of military jurisdiction set up by the Republic of Marzocco in 1384 in opposition to the city of Siena. Its purpose was to defend and administer the territory whose Florentine outposts were coveted by their Sienese rivals – today the communes of Castellina in Chianti, Gaiole in Chianti and Radda in Chianti.

But why choose a rooster? Tradition has it that during these medieval power struggles, Florence and Siena both claimed control over this valuable area of Tuscany and were ready to fight over it. But, wearying of their bloody battles, they decided on an original and peaceful method of arbitration to settle their differences.

In order to define the boundary of the disputed territory once and for all, the cities devised a contest between two knights, one representing Florence and the other Siena. The outcome would decide where the border was to be drawn between the two cities, on the spot where the two knights met after setting out on horseback from their respective cities at cockcrow. The Sienese chose a white rooster, which they stuffed with as many choice titbits as it could eat, convinced that would make it crow louder. The Florentines, on the other hand, chose a black rooster that they deliberately starved. On the day of the race, the hungry bird began to crow long before dawn, while the pampered white one, its crop full to bursting, slumbered on like the most peaceful creature in the world.

So the Florentine knight galloped off as soon as the cock crowed, while

the Sienese knight had to wait until his bird eventually roused itself. The two horsemen met scarcely 12 km from the walls of Siena, which gave the Florentine Republic the right to annex almost all the Chianti region. Today, the Chianti Classico consortium comprises the entire territory of the communes of Castellina in Chianti, Gaiole in Chianti, Greve in Chianti, Radda in Chianti and part of those of Barberino Val d'Elsa, Castelnuovo Berardenga, Poggibonsi, San Casciano in Val di Pesa and Tavarnelle Val di Pesa.

FORMER HOSPICE OF BIGALLO

A hotel in a former hospice

14, Via Bigallo e Apparita - 50012 Bagno a Ripoli
Visits by reservation at the Assessorato alla Cultura [Cultural Affairs Department] of Bagno a Ripoli
Tel: 055 63 90 356
Note that during the holiday season the first floor (used as hotel space) cannot be visited
Hotel Season: from 1 April to 30 September
Hotel Reservations: Casella Postale 25. San Donato in Poggio. 50028 Tavarnelle val di Pesa
Tel: 340.41.23.101. E-Mail: info@bigallo.it. www.bigallo.it/bigost_it.htm
Manager: Franco Lodini: 335 39 30 50
Rates (including breakfast): dormitory bed: 25 €; double room 39 € per person.
Directions: By car, leave the Firenze Sud motorway and follow the signs to Bagno a Ripoli right to the sign indicating "Ospedale del Bigallo." By bus, take the no. 33 from the station of Santa Maria Novella and get off at the La Fonte stop. It is then a 15-minute walk

Located on the road to Arezzo and affording a remarkable panoramic view of Florence, the former Bigallo Hospice provided hospitality and assistance to pilgrimages on their way to Rome. Founded in the 13th century and modelled on a number of such hospices that were dotted around Europe, the Bigallo has now been carefully restored and can give you a real feel of what things must have been like eight centuries ago.

During the tourist season, visits are restricted to the ground floor because the first floor is actually still used to provide accommodation to guests. The first of the two dormitories is reminiscent of the sort of place one sees in films set in old-fashioned hospitals, with lines of beds separated from each other by a simple curtain. The other dormitory is a faithful reproduction of what the hospice was like at the time of the pilgrims; it is lined with a double podium on which mattresses are laid out.

There are also five double rooms with en-suite bathrooms.

At the time of printing, still undergoing restoration, the ground floor has an attractive painted coffered ceiling. Halfway up the wall you can still see the rounded recess where a monk recited prayers during meals. The kitchen, which is open to visitors, is a spectacular sight with its fireplace, chimney canopy and stone sinks.

The rural charm of the site and the spectacular views it affords make this a wonderful place to stay.

THE FOUNTAIN OF FATA MORGANA

A fountain of eternal youth?

Corner of Via delle Fonti and Via di Fattucchia - 50012 Bagno a Ripoli
Directions: By car, turn off the Firenze Sud motorway and follow the signs to Greve in Chianti until you reach a place called Grassina. Follow Via delle Fonti, at the beginning of which there is a signpost to the fountain, which stands at the far end of the street.
Visits by reservation only: Assessorato alla Cultura di Bagno a Ripoli (tel: 055 63 90 356) or Cooperativa per i Servizi Culturali Megaton (tel: 055 48 04 89)
Admission: 2.60 €, reduced: 1.30 €
The building can be viewed from outside, but the interior and main fountain are shut behind gates

The Fountain or Nymphaeum* of Fata Morgana (*Ninfeo della Fata Morgana*) is an astonishing building imbued with a dreamlike atmosphere of myth and, perhaps, magic.

According to an inscription carved in stone**, the waters of this fountain are recognised as bestowing youth upon those who drink it. The unusual and mysterious look of the place has encouraged legends and stories: it is said that bacchanals were held here on summer nights, with beautiful young nymphs and fairies then disappearing just as suddenly as they had appeared. The whole structure was part of the gardens of the Villa Il Riposo which was built in the 15th century (it is also known as Villa Vecchietti, after the family who purchased the property in 1515).

The grounds were not enclosed at the time as the fountain was originally intended for public use… in particular for the peasants working on the estate. Probably designed by Giambologna, the building is flanked by a tabernacle that dates from 1573-1574 and has two drinking-fountains and a water-trough for animals.

The central fountain is known as Il Fonte del Viandante [Fountain of the Traveller] because it was available to any passers-by. The basin is surmounted by a strange sculpture of a gorgon, which is said to depict Fata Morgana. The body of the building gives access to the main fountain. This has a shell-shaped basin supported by two mermaids. The niche above it is rather bare as another statue of Fata Morgana – also the work of Giambologna – has now disappeared.

Fata Morgana

According to legend, Fata Morgana was King Arthur's sister (or half-sister), also known as Morgan le Fay. She tried to resist the growing power of Christianity within Brittany, which was largely due to the influence of the very pious Queen Gweniver. Ancient beliefs were the basis of her own magical powers, as they were at the basis of the powers wielded by Merlin. It was Morgana who is said to have embroidered the magical scabbard for Excalibur, which protected Arthur from any fatal wound in combat.

---

* *In Roman times a nymphaeum was a monumental public fountain adorned with sculpture and jets of waters. It was made up of one or more basins backed by a multi-level ornamental façade. There were also private nymphaea, for example in Pompeii. Originally, the term came from Greek and referred to a sanctuary dedicated to the nymphs.*

** *"I am, o reader, the youthful Fata Morgana, who here gives youth to others…."*

STATUE OF FIDO

*After the death of his owner, Fido waited at
the same spot for 14 years...*

Piazza Dante
50032 Borgo San Lorenzo (FI)

C uriously, the main square in Borgo San Lorenzo features the statue of a dog, which bears the inscription "To Fido, an example of fidelity." The story began when Carlo Soriano found a wounded and abandoned dog that he gave the typical name of "Fido." Unfortunately, their time together was cut short when Carlo was killed during a bombing raid on 30 December 1943. From that day onwards, Fido would for fourteen years (that is, more than 5,000 days) continue to go to the bus stop of Luco del Mugello to await his owner's return from work at the factory.

A campaign started by a journalist would ultimately lead to the town's mayor presenting Fido with a Gold Medal in a ceremony held on 9 November 1957 in the presence of Carlo Soriano's widow. Fido died on 9 June 1958 and was buried alongside his master.

NEARBY

Crucifix in the oratory of the Sanctissimo Crocifisso di Miracoli ㉗

Piazza G. Pecori Giraldi
50032 Borgo San Lorenzo (FI)
The Crucifix is displayed on every Friday in Lent, on Easter Sunday and the first Sunday of each month.
For further information, phone 055 84 59 088

Undoubtedly the work of the 14th century sculptor Giovanni Pisano, this painted wood crucifix is, as the name of the oratory suggests, miraculous. Located in a niche above the main altar it is usually hidden by a painting by the 19th century artist Giuseppe Bezzuoli and is only rarely put on display (see dates above), with the painting being raised by a special mechanism.

In the 15th century a group of German pilgrims who had bought the wooden crucifix to take to Rome were caught up in an outbreak of the plague and had to leave it behind in Borgo San Lorenzo. This Cross was then acquired by a confraternity of flagellants and soon became renowned for its miraculous powers. Initially housed at the premises of the confraternity, it was later moved to this oratory, which was built over the period 1714-1743. Amongst other things, the crucifix is credited with having put an end to an outbreak of the plague in the fifteenth century, with the fact that the village suffered only slight damage during the earth tremors of 1542 (however, after the 1919 earthquake, the oratory did have to be entirely rebuilt) and, finally, with the end of the French occupation in 1799.

GROTTA DEL ROMITO

A spring capable of quenching spiritual thirst?

50034 Marradi
Directions: after passing the Marradi conurbation in the direction of Florence, continue as far as Biforco, then take the bridge over the Lamone River. Follow the signs for Campigno and go up the road for a few minutes until you reach a place called Albero, with some small villas dotted among lush greenery. You then continue on foot, via the white dirt road that climbs gently, bordered by groves of chestnut trees and, after rounding a bend, leads into a wood where a noticeboard indicates the way to Romito's grotto. Cross two wooden bridges, climb up a little further, and after around an hour's walk an overhanging wall of tuff comes into view, weather-worn over the millennia. Inside you'll see a small cave – this is Romito's grotto.

The legends that grew up around Romito's grotto claim that it was formed by a meteorite that fell millions of years ago.

A number of hermits chose this site as their spiritual home and place of meditation, among them the Camaldolese (Benedictine monastic community) monk, the Blessed Pietro da Portico, also known as Pietro Candido. Around the year 1000, the Blessed Piero San Romualdo and San Pietro Damiano also lived there. We do not know if the attraction is due to its extraterrestrial origin, or the spiritual strength and energy left behind by the various hermits who chose to meditate here, but this grotto is now a place of pilgrimage for believers and non-believers alike. Inside are a small wooden altar, crosses, statuettes, sacred images, some spartan seats and votive offerings, as well as handwritten prayers and wishes placed in niches in the rock or hung on the tuff walls – a place that lends itself to spiritual peace and deep meditation.

Some visitors claim that the scent of violets and incense is often noticeable. Since the year 1000, a spring has also flowed there – the water is said to be able to quench spiritual thirst.

In 1988, thanks to the dedication of a local man, the grotto and the path leading to it were rescued from their neglected state and cleared of the ever-more invasive undergrowth. This man claimed to have been commanded to do so in a dream, to allow pilgrims to find their inner path.

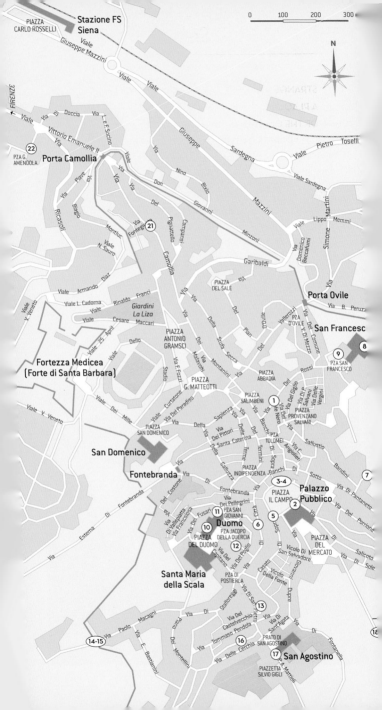

Siena

STRANGE "LAMPPOST" IN VIA DEL ① REFE NERO

A head on a spike in a cage

21, Via del Refe Nero - 53100 Siena (SI)

At No. 21 Via del Refe Nero there is a very mysterious sight: a severed head fixed on a spike and enclosed within a cage of wrought iron. This macabre decoration was set up by the previous owner, the Sienese antiquarian Giuseppe Mazzoni. In effect, he restructured this entire Palazzo del Diavolo Rosso [Palace of the Red Devil] in the 1930s, giving it a rather fanciful neo-medieval appearance.

Mazzoni was an eccentric character who inherited from his father, another passionate collector, the family business of Casa d'Arte Antica Senese, which had been founded in 1880. After his retirement, Giuseppe Mazzoni would acquire a certain notoriety in the 1950s when, in Il Giornale dell'Antiquario [The Antique Dealer's Journal], he published an account of the role he had played in selling the "works" of the gifted forger Icilio Federico Joni (1866-1946).

A forger of genius

Between 1890 and 1918, Icilio Federico Joni would manage to pass off a number of his own creations as the works of such 14th and 15th century Sienese masters as Duccio, Lorenzetti and Martini. Even experts of the calibre of Bernard Berenson were taken in by his almost perfect copies.

A foundling, Joni had been raised at the Santa Maria della Scala orphanage. His autobiography Le Memorie di un pittore di quadri antichi [Memoirs of a Painter of Old Masters] was published in 1932. Even though it disguised the names of the dealers who had sold his paintings, it had an enormous impact, creating uncertainty for all the private individuals and public institutions that had purchased a work by the Siena Primitives during the period when Icilio Federico Joni was active as a forger.

NEARBY

A plaque commemorating the reform of the calendar ②

Façade of the Palazzo Pubblico - Piazza del Campo - 53100 Siena (SI)

On 20 November 1749, the Grand Duke of Tuscany decreed that, from 1 January the following year, there was to be one uniform calendar used within his duchy. Known as the "modern style" [stile moderno] calendar, it replaced the "incarnation calendars" that had previously been used in Pisa and Florence. These latter not only celebrated the New Year on 23 March (the Feast of the Annunciation; hence the reference to "incarnation"), but also were also at variance with one another: the Pisan calendar was 9 months and 7 days ahead of the "modern" version, while the Florentine calendar lagged 2 months and 24 days behind. At the time of the reform, Siena was using the Florentine calendar.

THE SECRETS OF THE PIAZZA DEL CAMPO

There's always something new to see

Piazza del Campo - 53100 Siena (SI)

The Piazza del Campo is one of the most famous places in the world. But scratch below the surface and you will see that there are things you could easily miss, and some of them need a little explanation even if they are in open view. An example of a classic photo of Siena is that of the Torre del Mangia, taken looking down the Chiasso del Bargello, perfectly framed on either side by the walls of buildings in the narrow alley. It is almost as if the early architects had deliberately created these views of the Piazza. But that is not the case. In a bedroom in one of the private houses that run along the chiasso stands an enormous doorway with a lancet arch. It can no longer be seen from outside because it was bricked up on the occasion of a papal visit. The alley was moved so that the pope, as he progressed down the hill from the cathedral along the Via di Città, could see the Torre to remind him that in Siena, power was shared between two people. Famously, since the Middle Ages, the Piazza del Campo has been regularly transformed into a horse racing track on the occasion of the Palio. Certain signs of this colourful metamorphosis can be seen at any time in the Piazza, although they are not immediately obvious. First of all, you will see hooks sticking out above the façades of some of the palazzi. These are used in the construction of the made-to-measure grandstands at the time of the Palio. Each element is designed to fit exactly into the space intended for it. Individual supporting poles can only fit into the specific holes designed to fit them. And at the end of the event the holes are covered over by stone 'lids', designed only to fit over its corresponding hole. Hence these numbered stones in various places in the Piazza. The palio, a sort of long flag which goes to the winner, is displayed in the square prior to the race. It is suspended on the corner of the Costarella dei Barbieri. On one occasion the palio was so heavy that it required a pulley to hoist it up. The pulley remains there, just in case...

Why are there not more balconies overlooking the square?

If intricately designed grandstands have to be erected and taken back down twice a year for people to watch the Palio, why are there not more balconies? The answer lies in the fact that in the old days, balconies were not built as an outdoor extended living space. The raised 'balconies' you see around the square were actually used as external passageways and commonly referred to 'landings'. You will see that these long walkways run along the first floor just above the businesses below. In fact, they run almost all the way round the square, except for two palazzi, which were built or rebuilt after the Middle Ages. The purpose of the walkways was to allow merchants to move more easily between warehouses. The Piazza del Campo sits in a conch shell-shaped hollow so that even today, the shop fronts are still on the ground floor — although strange as it may seem, not in the Piazza del Campo but in the main street behind it.

PRIVATE COLLECTION OF BOTTLES ④
OF WINE AND LIQUEUR
The history of Italy and design through alcohol

A stone's throw from the Piazza del Campo - 53100 Siena (SI)
Visits by appointment
Tel: 338-698-010 - Email: fromsiena@alice.it
www.ilpalio.org/liquori_italia.htm

When you enter this rather idiosyncratic living room set in the cellar of an historic *palazzo,* a stone's throw from the Piazza del Campo, you will be charmed. It is in a private house, the central focus of which is on meditation and a collection that its owner will be happy to show to anyone ready and willing to appreciate the experience.

The impressive collection consists of about 1,500 bottles of wine and liqueur, all of which are full and their seals intact. They tell the history of Italy, starting with a bottle of 1907 Castello di Brolio chianti.

The collection has been passionately built up over more than forty years. At first it concentrated on wines produced in the region around Siena (a surprisingly wide selection), but has been extended to include a broad range of curiosities selected to reflect the history of the first half of the 20th century.

Among its other treasures, you will see a rare kosher chianti, two bottles of 1945 Brunello di Montalcino Biondi Santi, a wine from Rhodes and a rhubarb liqueur produced in Benghazi at the time when the island, like the rest of Libya, was an Italian colony.

There are outrageous imitations of Campari Cordial on show, brandies bottled in small returnable glass containers that the Allies imported into Italy during the war, as well as liqueurs with Italianised names dating from the twenty years of fascism, such as *curassò* (Curacao), *triplo secco* (triple sec), and *Archibugio* (Arquebuse liqueur). There are bottles in the form of mirrors, ashtrays, penguins and many other things besides.

Apart from the everyday liqueurs, the collection includes an array of speciality items that were in vogue at one time or another. Another interesting aspect of the collection is that it illustrates how the artwork on the labels has changed over the decades. Some labels are typewritten, many others are truly works of art, while some boast the most outrageous descriptions, promising some highly improbable health benefits.

Each bottle in the collection tells more than just its own story. And the collection itself provides a fascinating insight into what drinks were available to choose from and how drinkers' tastes have changed over the last hundred years.

But what makes this more than just an exhibition is the homely atmosphere of the room where it is displayed. It has been painstakingly recreated in retro style, forming the perfect place for the owner to chat with his friends and guests. Many of the bottles in the collection will doubtless never be opened. Nevertheless, they make a perfect backdrop for all the ones that do get opened in this place!

From the centre of Siena, a dip into the past

Access is through the gardens of the Contrada del Leocorno, accessible from Via Follonica; from the gate into the gardens, head down towards the bottom of the valley

Siena still draws its drinking water from a number of fountains (not springs), the histories of which are sometimes lost in the mists of time, as is the incredible network of rooms, passages and tunnels that extend under the ground on which the town sits. It is actually possible to cover a greater distance through these underground chambers than by travelling along the streets of Siena (see the box on the opposite page).

While the most aesthetically attractive fountain is undoubtedly Jacopo della Quercia's Fonte Gaia, it is essential to seek out the delightful Fonte di Follonica in Piazza del Campo, one of the biggest ones, albeit less well known than the Fonte Gaia. Three large Romanesque arches with cross-ribbed vaults remain for us to appreciate. They were intended to shelter the basins where people would come to drink in bygone ages. But they were also used by the *fullones* (washerwomen) and were conceived with their work in mind.

Although Follonica's water was located in the city walls, its source was in a valley that is difficult to reach. The fountain, a dozen or so metres high, was entirely buried until recently. It was located under a pile of detritus that had accrued from a succession of different building projects beginning as far back as the 16th century. It had been permanently abandoned after a final attempt to maintain it in 1493.

Visits to the spring have become sanitised now and are managed by the Contrada del Leocorno. They provide a story within the story of Siena, and as you descend into the little valley where the spring is located you are truly on a journey lost in time. It is hard to believe that you are less than 200 metres from the Piazza del Campo as the crow flies, in this place where the only things left are watchtowers on the ramparts, trees, meadows and ancient springs from which clean drinking water still flows.

There is a strange story told about this place, intended to discourage children from going to the fountain after centuries of its neglect. The tale describes how a washerwoman, after losing a child there, put a curse on the spring, causing it to become buried under the earth. The ghost of this woman is still supposed to haunt this place as she awaits the return of a knight, the father of the child that disappeared.

When this spring was reclaimed, plans included the construction of a little amphitheatre facing the fountain. But the facility is rarely used, except when the Contrada del Leocorno holds two or three theatrical performances there every year (see page 75).

Underground Siena and the search for the imaginary river

Siena is built on a hill. There are no rivers or springs close by. So where does the water (drinkable, no less!) that gushes abundantly from the town's fountains come from? The answer is from under the ground, which has been transformed by man over the millennia. Documents provide evidence that people have been excavating below the surface of the town in search of water since 394 A.D. For centuries people have been searching for the mythical River Diana, said to cross the centre of the town from north-east to south-west. So much effort and money has been sacrificed on this project that Dante refers to it in his *Purgatory*, as if quoting a proverb, as an insane obsession with searching for something that doesn't exist. Nevertheless, centuries of digging has led to the creation of an exceptional network of underground ducts that capture water from very distant springs or simply fill up by a process of filtration of groundwater. Siena does indeed sit upon rock, which, due to its rich sand content (tuffeau stone), is very porous and makes an excellent natural filter. Rain falling on the rock's surface penetrates through it before being collected by cleverly constructed ducts known as *bottini*, which in turn bring the water to the town's fountains. There are at least 25 kilometres of underground tunnels below Siena. While some of them were constructed in the Middle Ages, others are certainly much older. What's more, it is not unusual to find Etruscan caves at depths of over 30 metres, sometimes directly under the town itself, which leads one to believe that hypogea have always existed there, along with the corridors that lead to them. A fine example of a perfectly preserved Etruscan room is the cellar of the *Le Logge* restaurant. If you ask the staff there or stop off at the counter of the *Un Tubo* bar, you will get the chance to immerse yourself in the past as you make your way down below street level.

For all information: Un Tubo, Via Luparello, 2. Tel: 0577-271-312. Email: circolo@untubo.it

LIBRARY AND CONCERT HALL OF ⑥ THE CHIGIANA MUSICAL ACADEMY

A musical treasure from the days of patronage

Palazzo Chigi Saracini, Via di Città, 89 - 53100 Siena (SI)
Open: The library opens Mon—Fri 8:30am—1:30pm and on Thursdays and Fridays 3:30pm—7pm. In July and August opening hours are longer and the library also opens on Saturdays.
The concert hall can be visited during guided tours of the palazzo. Visits Mon—Sat from 11:30am and on Thursdays and Fridays at 4pm. Entrance fee is 7€.
In July and August, opening hours vary in accordance with teaching requirements. Visits are not available in September.
www.chigiana.it

The Palazzo Chigi Saracini stands right in the centre of town, but there are lots of hidden surprises to discover within, starting with its music library, which is open every day to the public.

The library holds roughly 75,000 volumes, some of which are the fruit of the collection handed down by the Chigi Saracini family. Other acquisitions relate to the advance musical study activities of the academy. The collection was created by Count Guido Chigi Saracini in 1932 and remains a reference library for professional classical musicians. Included in the library are some very rare works, such as illuminated manuscripts, first editions and of particular note, original musical scores dedicated to the Count, a true patron of music. The most famous of these is without doubt the Suite della Tabacchiera by Ottorino Respighi, who composed it having been inspired by the musical design decorating a tobacco box belonging to the Count. Even before the creation of the advanced music school, the Count's passion for music inspired him to make radical changes to the medieval layout of certain rooms of his *palazzo* and create a Viennese-style concert hall. The hall can hold more than two hundred people, but the Count himself preferred to listen to the performances from a salon through a door to the left of the stage. The Count enjoyed playing the organ, which prompted him to have a magnificent organ built for himself. This formed the basis for the creation of the advanced music classes.

Although it is partly concealed behind the walls, which extend over two floors of the *palazzo*, the stately organ, with its set of about 4,200 pipes, can be seen from the concert hall. This fine instrument has attracted many musicians, among them Fernando Germani, the founder of the first advanced music classes for the organ.

Students practice in the enormous rooms of the *palazzo*, which contain some amazing items from the Count's collection. It is good to be reminded of him by a visit to the *palazzo*, or in summer when you can hear the music from the streets outside it.

THE CONTRADA DEL LEOCORNO ⑦ MUSEUM

Much more than the history of the Palio

Piazzetta Virgilio Grassi, Siena (access via the Church of San Giovannino dell Staffa Open: Daily 4:30pm—7pm. If the museum is closed call mobile number 3478-803-657
Free entry (donations welcome)

The *contrada* (urban district) of Il Leocorno — one of the largest in the area but perhaps the least populated — has decided to allow everybody access to its treasures, its church and its museum on a day to day basis. That was not an easy decision to take when you think about what a *contrada* is and how it operates. All the work and meticulous devotion on which the very existence of the *contrade* depends could not be achieved without the *contradaioli* — people who voluntarily give up their time and money to their area.

As well as a museum, each *contrada* has its own church and a baptismal font, where, just before the Palio starts, the horse selected for the rider is blessed. Each is also allocated an enormous space to be shared among the people who live there and their guests. The museum houses banners, costumes, documents and items relating to the centuries-old history of the *contrada*. The different *palii* (banners) that the *contrada* has won over the course of its history are on display. Each *palio* is a unique work of art — and the only tangible proof of the *contrada* having won the famous horse race.

The iconography of the Palio has changed dramatically over the centuries, but from the beginning of the 20th century a truly remarkable period of creativity has developed, not only in terms of the graphic art itself but also in the fascinating presentation of this local (and indeed international) history. One after the other, some very famous painters have brought the Palio to life, and they continue to do so. Two different pictures are painted every year and these works remain unique and unequalled.

Visiting museums of different *contrade* can prove tricky, but if you turn up in the evening full of interest in the area, it is highly likely that somebody will open the doors and light up the rooms for you. These museums are exceptional, not only for the collections they house, but also for the way they are laid out, being designed by a *contradaiolo* architect and maintained by a *contradaiolo* historian or archivist.

A CHRIST WITH MOVEABLE ARMS ⑧

A Christ with moving limbs

Basilica of San Francesco
Piazza San Francesco
53100 Siena (SI)
Opening hours: 7.30-12.00 and 15.30-19.00
In winter, closed from "around" 19.00
Free admission

There are not many existing statues of Christ with moving arms and limbs; most of them were suppressed by the ecclesiastical authorities during the period of the Reformation and, particularly, the Counter-Reformation. The majority of such statues were medieval in origin and had been used primarily during Holy Week, when they figured in realistic enactments of the Deposition from the Cross (a episode of Christ's Passion that was known in Italy as Il Mortorio). Such enactments were even more popular in Spain and can still be seen today in some countries of South America: at San Andres Sajeabaja in Guatemala, for example, a Christ with moveable limbs is removed from the Cross each Good Friday and laid out in a glass coffin. The main feature of these figures is an articulated shoulder joint. This means the arms can be raised when fixing Christ to the Cross, and then hang limp after the nails are removed. A further advantage was that the arms could be raised to any angle, so that the body could be adapted to any type of cross.

There is no precise information as to the origin or date of this particular example of a Christ with moveable arms. Possibly it is contemporary with that in the church of San Pietro de Pieve in Presciano (Valdarno), which has been dated from the 15th century. Note that the figure of Christ in Presciano may be difficult to see, as the church there is only open for mass and other religious services.

NEARBY
The heraldic arms of the Tolomei family ⑨

Entering the cloister to the right of the basilica, if you turn left and walk to the far end you come to a staircase whose steps are adorned with

a number of little coats-of-arms: however, you need good eyesight to make them out. Tradition has it that these eighteen identical crests of the Tolomei commemorate the eighteen members of that family who were murdered in the 14th entury during the course of a meal held at a villa in Via Cassia; the event was supposed to ark their reconciliation with the Salimbeni family. This tragic episode would lead to the entire area becoming known as Malamerenda from the Italian words for evil/bad [male] and meal/refreshment [merenda].

MAGIC SQUARE IN THE CATHEDRAL

Secret identity codes for the first Christians

Siena Cathedral
Piazza del Duomo - 53100 Siena (SI)
www.operaduomo.siena.it/

On the left side of the cathedral, on practically the last part of the wall that is visible, there is a strange square formed of five Latin words carved into a slab of white marble. Arranged one word per line, these form a palindrome which reads:

SATOR AREPO TENET OPERA ROTAS

Read left to right, right to left, upwards or downwards, this arrangement of letters always forms the same sentence: *Sator arepo tenet opera rotas*. There are some doubts about the meaning of *arepo*, but the two translations for the entire phrase most widely accepted are: "The Sower takes care of his plough and his work" or "The Labourer guiding the plough works by turning around." All sorts of esoteric, religious, alchemical, numerological and cabbalistic interpretations of these sentences have been put forward; however, the hypothesis that the stone is somehow linked with the Templars became untenable when, in 1936, a similar stone palindrome was found on a column in the amphitheatre of Pompeii, the Roman city buried by an eruption of Vesuvius in 79 AD.

Nevertheless, a Christian explanation of its origin still seems to be the most plausible one, with this square of words being used by the early Christians as a code whereby they could recognise each other. Note, for example, that the square contains a central cross made up of the word TENET, flanked at top and bottom by the letters A and O, Alpha and Omega. What is more, one can form a cross with the 25 letters and form the words Pater noster twice, without using the A and the O twice... It could be that these palindromes or "magic squares" or "holy squares" were intended to drive the forces of evil away from the cathedral (a function similar to that of the labyrinth at the cathedral of Lucca, see page 152).

```
        P
        A
A       T       O
        E
        R
PATERNOSTER
        O
        S
O       T       A
        E
        R
```

Such magic squares are to be found in about a dozen places in Italy, most notably at Campiglia Marittima outside Livorno (see page 241), at the Palazzo Benciolini in Verona and in Urbino.

SHAFTS FROM THE MONTAPERTI "VICTORY CHARIOT"

Two unusual reminders of the battle of Montaperti inside the Cathedral

Cathedral of Santa Maria Assunta, Piazza del Duomo
53100 Siena (SI)

Placed vertically behind the fifth columns in the nave of the cathedral are two reminders of the famous victory of Montaperti (see below). They look just like two poles of wood, but they are in fact the shafts from the Victory Chariot (carroccio) and were placed here as an offering of thanks to the Madonna degli Occhi Grossi [Madonna of the Large Eyes] that then stood on the high altar of the cathedral. (It is now to be seen in the Museo dell'Opera Metropolitana, a short distance away).

On the eve of the battle, the entire city went in solemn procession with this carroccio to invoke the protection of the Madonna. Indeed, the very survival of the vehicle after the battle was itself a sort of miracle. It had been entrusted to the Luccan troops led by Niccolò da Bigozzi, who were thrown into disarray when their captain was impaled by the German knight Gualtieri d'Astimbergh. In the ensuing confusion, Bigozzi's troops became involved in the battle itself and forgot their orders to protect the venerated carroccio.

The battle of Montaperti

The battle of Montaperti was the culmination of the war between Siena and Florence in the 13th century, when economic and political rivalry made a clash between the two cities inevitable. Furthermore, Florence was a Guelph city supporting the Papacy, whilst Siena was Ghibelline and supported the Holy Roman Emperor.

The casus belli exploited by the Florentines on this occasion was the fact that Siena had given refuge to the Ghibellines who had just been driven out of Florence. The battle took place on 4 September 1260. Over the years, accounts of the battle became more legendary than factual, attributing the Sienese victory to feats of arms that are still the subject of discussion and debate.

The term "Guelph" comes from the name of the German dynasty of the Welfs. It refers to the faction who supported the pope in opposition to the Holy Roman Emperor. The term "Ghibelline" comes from the name of the castle of Waiblingen in Germany, the seat of the Hohenstaufen dynasty, who struggled to establish themselves on the throne of the Holy Roman Empire.

MARKS OF GUNFIRE
ON THE NEW CATHEDRAL

A 14th century marble wall riddled with bullet holes

Facciatone
Piazza Jacopo della Quercia - 53100 Siena (SI)

On the imposing facade of the (unfinished) new cathedral, there are dozens of bullet holes in the marble. Siena was liberated on 3 July 1944, but in the last days of June a plane (no one knew if it was American or German) made several low passes here, strafing the area around the cathedral. Many of the bullets then ricocheted off the ground and hit the façade of the church. It was later discovered that the pilot was actually from Siena (he lived in Via di Rossi) and had wanted to demonstrate that the Fascist army still had the power to strike back.

A welcome less warm than it seems...

The arch over the Camolia gateway bears the welcoming inscription Cor magis tibi Sena pandit [Siena opens its heart to you even wider than its gates], which was carved there in honour of Ferdinando I de Medici when he visited the city. The phrase figures in all the tourist books, but most of the local people know that it was far from being a spontaneous expression of welcome... Cosimo I, known in Siena as the "Medicean thief," had just robbed the city of its liberty...

NEARBY
The Madonna of the Crow ⑬
2, Via del Castelvecchio - 53100 Siena (SI)

At the corner of Via Stalloreggi and Via del Castelvecchio is a tabernacle with frescoes by Giovanni Antonio Bazzi , known as Il Sodoma*. A pietà, with the Virgin holding the dead Christ in her arms, the fresco is known in Siena as The Madonna of the Crow. The name itself dates from 1348, when a crow that fell dead in front of the tabernacle was taken as a presage of the arrival in Siena of the plague that had been raging in Europe for almost a year.

The Black Death would in fact soon arrive from Pisa, being particularly virulent in the months from April to October 1348. The Sienese chronicler Agnolo di Tura described it as "the worst, the grimmest and most horrible that the city has known. Everyone expected to die. The church bells no longer rang. It was the end of the world..." He himself lost his five children during the outbreak.

It was ultimately impossible to count the number of victims; but it is estimated that two-thirds of a population of 100,000 were affected.

* Sodoma's nickname was a mocking reference to his taste for youths...

THE NATIONAL ANTARCTIC MUSEUM

A little piece of Mars!

Via del Laterino, 8 - 53100 Siena (SI)
Open: Mon—Fri 9am—1pm; Tue—Thurs 3pm—5pm
Tel: 0577-233-777 - Email: mna@unisi.it
www.mna.it

The Italian National Antarctic research program was inaugurated in 1985. From 1997 it was decided that all the rocks found there should be studied and held at the University of Siena, which continues to carry out work on their classification in their laboratories specialising in rock slicing, analysis and examination under optical microscopes.

This ever-expanding collection eventually mutated into this museum where the most scientifically noteworthy discoveries are on display; primitive rocks that have remained unchanged for more than two billion years, *ventifatti* (rock 'sculptures' that owe their form exclusively to the extreme polar winds), as well as fossilised leaves and tree trunks, which prove that the southern continent was once very different from what it has become today.

Another no less important part of the museum is dedicated to some even more extraordinary phenomena, if that is possible — meteorites. Because of its natural cycles, Antarctica is an ideal place to find them. What's more, you can even gaze upon a piece of Mars in Siena!

The museum's explanatory panels provide us with information on the indigenous animal life of Antarctica, as well as describing some of the most noteworthy natural phenomena to be found on this continent. We are informed through text and images about the day-to-day lives of researchers both today and in the past. Visitors are even given the opportunity to try on their specialised clothing. Not exactly spacesuits, but not too different either! There is also a library in the museum containing texts and geological maps of the Antarctic going back to 1812. The original expedition logbooks of pioneers such as Scott and Shackleton are particularly noteworthy.

NEARBY
The Earth Science Museum ⑮

Located in the university building opposite the Antarctic Museum, this fine museum only opens by appointment. It consists of seventeen thematic display cases situated in corridors spread over three floors of the university. Each is dedicated to a specific geological field. For information and guided tours (free and conducted by the university) contact museodiscienzedellaterra@unisi.it or phone 0577-233-838 and ask for Professor Giancarlo Pagani.

NEARBY

The ghost in the Botanical Garden (16)

50, Via della Cerchia - 53100 Siena (SI)

The curious marble head embedded in the wall of the house at 50, Via della Cerchia is said to be a portrait bust of the painter Giacomo del Sodoma, known as Giomo (1507-1562), who is not to be confused with Giovanni Antonio Bazzi, known as Il Sodoma (1477-1549). Popular tradition links this bust with the ghost which made nocturnal appearances in the Botanical Gardens at the beginning of the 20th century. In his Toscanissima (Edizioni Bonecchi), Giorgio Batini claims, however, that the head is that of "the hermit of Porta dell'Arco," a young nobleman who fought against the Florentines at the battle of Montalcino in 1176. Seriously wounded during that defeat, he is said to have recovered after a long convalescence, at the end of which he decided to abandon military glory for life as a hermit at the city gateway of Porta all'Arco. However, when the Sienese marched out to fight again in 1207, he joined them, only to be killed during the first skirmishes with the Florentines. On 9 November 1952, this ghostly visage would once more be the subject of talk – when the bust in Via della Cerchia disappeared. One evening, perhaps after a drink too many over dinner, the members of the Contrada de la Tartuca [tortoise] had decided they wanted to take a closer look at this symbolic head. The street being badly lit, they took it home with them so as to be able to see it properly. Then they forgot to put it back, and the press got hold of the story. However, the "Hermit of Porta dell'Arco" was then discreetly returned to its niche – and the furore soon subsided.

16 June 1794: a hail of meteorites on Siena

At 7pm on 16 June 1794 meteorites rained down on the south-eastern part of the city of Siena. It was the first time in recorded history that such a shower had fallen within an urban area, making it possible for the phenomenon to be studied. The meteorites were preceded by a dense cloud issuing plumes of smoke and slow gleams of red lightning. Those which struck the ground varied in weight from a few hundred milligrams to three kilos. There were numerous eyewitnesses, including a number of English tourists (already!). The event then attracted sightseers as well as scientists from all over Italy, who wanted to collect testimonies before putting forward any explanations. Just 18 hours after this meteorite shower, the volcano Vesuvius erupted. The scientific community was divided into two camps, between those who thought the two events were connected and those who did not; the volcano is, after all, 450 kilometres from Siena. By an incredible coincidence, just two months before the meteorites fell, the German physicist Ernst Chaladni had published his *The Origin of Ferrous Rocks*, in which he argued that they could have fallen out of the sky. The publication of this work in Great Britain – together with the fall of a rock weighing 30 kg in Yorkshire and eyewitness accounts from those who might earlier have kept quiet for fear of being ridiculed – helped to advance serious scientific study of meteorites.

THE NATURAL HISTORY MUSEUM OF ⑰ THE ACCADEMIA DEGLI FISIOCRITICI*

The atmosphere of a wunderkammer

2, Piazzetta Silvio Gigli - 53100 Siena (SI)
Tel. : 0577 47 002
E-mail : fisiocritici@unisi.it - www.accademiafisiocritici.it
Opening hours: Monday - Friday 9.00-14.00
Free admission

ounded more than 300 years ago, the Academy of the Physiocritics has various collections which form a museum with a distinct 19th century charm. Since 1816 this has been housed in a 12th century monastery, with its numerous remarkable exhibits divided between three main sections: geological, zoological and anatomical. At the centre of the cloister, for example, is the skeleton of a 15-metre whale which became beached near Piombino in 1974.

In the geological section, be sure not to miss the collection of ancient marbles. The 230 samples come from buildings not only in Rome and the surrounding area but from all the various regions of the Roman Empire. The section also includes one of the world's most famous meteorites, known as the "Siena Meteorite:" this chondrite (the name indicates a meteorite of which at least 35% is made up of metals) was one of those which fell on the city in the famous meteorite storm of 16 June 1794 (see previous double page).

Among the other curiosities of this fascinating museum are the display cases of monsters, including two-headed lambs and sheep. Under a black cloth cover there is even part of the coat of a mammoth found frozen in Siberia. Moving into the screening room, one also finds a magnificent meridian now laid out under the spectators' seats. The work of Giuseppe Pianigiani, this is a detailed reconstruction of the original designed and created in 1703 by the founder of the Academy, Pirro Maria Gabrielli. At the time, this meant that Siena was one of only four cities with such an instrument (the others being Paris, Rome and Bologna). The instrument worked in this way: a guardian used to watch for the exact passage of a ray of sunlight along the axis of the meridian and then immediately have the bell (in the Torre della Mangia) rung to announce noon. The sundial was even used to correct mechanical clocks. Known as the "Physiocritic Heliometre," it was unfortunately destroyed during an earthquake in 1798.

* *The word "physiocritic" comes from the Greek words physis (Nature) and kritikos (he who studies).*

PALAZZO GALGANO

A metal ring that recalls something

47, Via Roma - 53100 Siena (SI)

With reference to the Abbey of Galgano and the sword in the stone (see page 97), the rings at Palazzo Galgano to which riders used to tie their horses are modelled on that famous sword; they, too, appear to be sunk into the stone. In fact, the palazzo was built for the monks from that abbey in 1474, when what is now Via Roma was called Via Maddalena.

NEARBY

The rusty plaques of the old psychiatric hospital

56, Via Roma
53100 Siena (SI)

Easy to make out thanks to the monumental portal that stands at the beginning of Via Roma, the old psychiatric hospital now houses part of the university. However, there are some extant traces of the città della follia [city of madness] that was once located here. Founded at the end of the 19th century, the hospital applied the theories of its day, which saw work as the essential basis for the treatment of mentally ill patients. It was laid out as a small town, with streets, workshops and shops – a "protected space" within which the inmates were allowed to move freely. Today, one still finds here and there a rusty plaque indicating the name of street or the presence of a tobacconist's.

Marcovaldo's Virgin and Child

Basilica di Santa Maria dei Servi
Piazza Alessandro Manzoni - 53100 Siena (SI)

The altarpiece in the second chapel along the south wall of the basilica was painted in 1261 by Coppo di Marcovaldo (1225-1265) and depicts The Virgin and Child with Two Angels. The circumstances in which this was created are worth mentioning. Fighting on the Florentine side in the battle of Montaperti in 1260 (see page 81), Coppo di Marcovaldo was taken prisoner by the Sienese. As he had no money to ransom himself, he was offered a deal which, tradition has it, was proposed in this terse exchange:

"What can you do?...Paint?... So paint!"

And this was how Coppo di Marcovaldo's only signed work comes to be found in the Basilica dei Servi.

MUSEUM OF THE CONFRATERNITÀ ㉑ DI SANTA MARIA IN PORTICO

The trophies of Christopher Columbus

Via Fontegiusta
53100 Siena (SI)
Visits by appointment only: phone Silvano Carletti at 347 181 31 14.
Admission is free, but a contribution to the costs of maintaining and restoring the church is appreciated
Church of Santa Maria in Portico
Mass each weekday at 8.00, open until noon; Saturday open at 17.00 with mass at 18.30; Sunday mass at 10.30

A discreet little place with no public signs to announce its presence, the museum of the Confraternità di Santa Maria in Portico is one of the gems of Siena. It can be visited only by appointment, when you enjoy an informed guided tour in the company of Silvano Carletti, a passionate student of his city's art and history. Along with priestly robes, ancient church furnishings, and other precious objects that are here protected against theft, one will also find four mementoes which, tradition has it, were offered by Christopher Columbus himself while still a student at Siena University. Said to have fallen in love with a young woman who was a parishioner of Fontegiusta, the young man presented the church with a painted wooden shield, an arquebus butt, a helmet, and sword – all of them supposed to be trophies from the battle of Poggio Imperiale fought against the Florentines in 1479.

The museum also has other curiosities relating to the life of the confraternity. These include some black and white beans which are over 200 years old and were found recently in an old coffer. The beans were not to be eaten but served as markers when the confraternity Council voted: a white bean meant "yes," a black one "no."

> The museum and the church after which it is named are often referred to by the name of the district, Fontegiusta, which itself is named after a drinking fountain. The objects described above once hung in the church itself, just below the oculus of the façade. All that remains there now is the spectacular whale bone, which was also donated by Christopher Columbus

NEARBY

Column commemorating the meeting of Frederick III and Eleanor of Portugal

The curious column in Piazza Amedola commemorates the remarkable episode of the first meeting between Frederick III, Holy Roman Emperor, and his betrothed, Eleanor, Infanta of Portugal. The two had never seen each other before, and this meeting was organised by the then bishop of Siena, Enea Silvio Piccolomini, later Pope Pius II (see Pienza pages 112-113). Remarkably, Pinturrichio's fresco of the event in the Piccolomini Library within the cathedral already shows the presence of a commemorative column, although the encounter had only taken place a few years before...

Outside Siena

MUMMIFIED HANDS OF A THIEF

An unidentified mummy and a famous sword

Abbey of San Galgano and the Montesiepi Chapel
53012 Chiusdino (SI)
Free access to the abbey
The chapel is open from 9.30 to dusk
Free admission
Tel: 0577 75 67 38

One of the sights that no visitor to Tuscany should miss, the Abbey of San Galgano is famous the world over: the esoteric symbolism of the sword in the stone, the serene beauty of an abbey which now stands open to the sky, and the powerful legends associated with the place – all make this a "must" for lovers of the curious and the usual. The hermitage (eremo in Italian) where the body of St. Galgano lies is on the top of the small hill, while the most spectacular feature of the abbey – the sword in the stone – is now protected by a dome of plexiglas.

However, the most curious feature of the entire place is to be found in the chapel alongside this sword: a coffer of wrought iron whose contents are hidden from the eyes of the young and the sensitive by a deep red cloth. When you lift the covering, beneath it you'll see two mummified forearms, the hands twisted in pain. A panel under the coffer explains that these belonged to one of the three men who, in 1181, tried to steal San Galgano's sword. Not only did they fail to get the sword, but they fell victim to wolves who protected the saint's hermitage. Though the story strikes one as mythical, recent carbon-dating has shown that the limbs do in fact date from the 12th century, the era in which the saint lived.

The sword in the stone : the legend of saint Galgano

Galgano Guidotti (1148 – 1181) was born into a noble family in Chiusdino, the village which stands alongside the abbey. Initially he led a carefree and dissolute life, which was brought to an end when the angel Gabriel appeared to him, exhorting him to mend his ways. In 1180 Galgano became a Cistercian monk, and marked the rejection of his former life by breaking his sword against a rock. However, instead of shattering, the sword sank into the stone, becoming more like a cross than a weapon – a "transformation" which Galgano interpreted as a sign from God. He would then live the rest of his days as a hermit. There are those who doubt the authenticity of the sword now on display. But it might be best to keep such doubts from children...

GRAFFITI IN THE FORMER PSYCHIATRIC BUILDING OF SAN GIROLAMO

A masterpiece of Art Brut on the walls of a psychiatric hospital

Ferri Building - Borgata San Lazzaro
56048 Volterra (PI)

In the 1960s, Oreste Fernando Nannetti – who renamed himself "N.O.F.4" – created one of the world's masterpieces of Art Brut on the walls of the Ferri building in the old psychiatric hospital. Over a stretch of wall measuring 180x2m, Nannetti used the buckle of the belt from his patient's uniform to write – or, rather, draw – his "Book of Life." Whilst certain lines of the script are now indecipherable, most can be made out – even if they are as hermetic as the Etruscan script they so strangely resemble.

Born in Rome in 1927, Nannetti would die in 1994. A withdrawn and  taciturn person, he spoke to no one apart from a psychiatric nurse (Aldo Trafeli), who understood that Nannetti was not simply mad but rather devoting himself to an artistic project that lay well outside the usual realms of sanity. Nannetti worked so furiously on his scratchings that the dust from the stone caused serious damage to his eyes. Nowadays, his work is gradually disappearing and the old hospital buildings are threatened with redevelopment.

The treatment of mental patients and the work of NOF4' inspired the singer-songwriter Simone Cristicchi to write *Ti regalerò una rosa* [I will give you a rose], which won first prize at the 2007 San Remo Song Festival.

NEARBY
Medieval standard measures ③

Palazzo dei Priori, Piazza dei Priori. Porta San Francesco, Via S. Lino

In Volterra one can still see two traces of the systems of measurement used in medieval times. Incised horizontally upon the stone facade of Palazzo dei Priori is a standard measure of the canna volterrana (2.362 metres), a unit of measurement in use in the 13th century. On the inner wall to the right of the San Francesco gate – also known as the San Stefano or Pisan gate – is a standard canna pisana. Slightly longer than the canna volterrana, this is carved into the stone vertically here. These standard measures were used when there was any dispute between merchants and their customers.

④

A cannonball embedded in a façade

12, Via Franceschini - 56048 Volterra (PI)

At No. 12 Via Franceschini (formerly Via del Campanile) there is a cannonball embedded in the façade of a building. If asked, the locals say either that they know nothing about it or else describe it as "yet another Florentine cannonball."

Maximilian's Volterra candelabras are yet to be paid for

A private home, Palazzo Viti can however be visited, sometimes with amusing information and facts being supplied by Giovanna Viti, who still lives here. One should note that the family crest does not include the royal crown: Vittorio-Emanuele II was received here, but as the unifier of Italy rather than as a reigning sovereign. The Viti are staunchly republican aristocrats. In the first main room, known as the ballroom, there are two surprisingly large and magnificent alabaster candelabras. They were original made for the ill-fated Maximilian of Habsburg, who would – briefly – reign as Maximilian I, Emperor of Mexico. When he was executed in 1867, the candelabras had still not been paid for, causing substantial losses to a number of alabaster craftsmen in Volterra; Giuseppe Viti himself would be forced into bankruptcy partly because of this unpaid debt. There are also two display cases with a unique collection of the broth cups used by women who had just given birth; the broth in question was supposed to stimulate their milk for breast-feeding. Quite apart from these curiosities, Palazzo Viti is in itself a fascinating place – above all for those who have seen Luchino Visconti's Sandra, starring Claudia Cardinale and Jean Sorel. Palazzo Viti. 41, Via dei Sarti. Volterra. Tel: 0588 84 047. Opening hours: from 10.00-13.00 and 14.30-18.30 during the high season. Out of season, by appointment: call Consorzio Turistico Volterra (0588 86 099) or the palazzo itself (see number above). Admission: 4 €.

ANTHROPOMORPHIC EX-VOTOS AT THE SANCTUARY OF ROMITUZZO

*More than 5,000 macabre ex-votos on the walls
of a sanctuary*

*17, Via P. Burresi
53036 Poggibonsi (Siena)
Tel: 0577 93 80 71*

This amazing place takes its name from the female hermits that used to pray here in the 14th century (romituzzo means "little hermitage"). Initially a small tabernacle with an image of the Madonna stood on this spot, the chapel then being built in 1460. From the 16th century onwards an increasing number of miracles were attributed to the Madonna of Romituzzo, leading to the custom of placing anthropomorphic ex-votos here in thanks for grace received. Made of papier-mâché by the craftsmen of the Colle di Val d'Elsa, they depicted the part of the body which had been saved or cured thanks to the intercession of the Virgin.

Many of these ex-votos were destroyed during a fire in 1631; however, 5,125 still remain. Lining the walls of the chapel, they give the place a rather surrealistic air. The body parts include: 1,400 heads, 1,171 legs, 559 feet, 550 hands, 425 arms, 278 torsos and 192 faces. There are also 351 profiles and 182 babies.

Tuscany: the first State in the world to abolish the death penalty

Town Hall. 18, Via Campana. 53034 Colle di Val d'Elsa (Siena).
The plaque is on the right in the corridor leading from the entrance to the ground-floor hall. It was unveiled on 30 November 2000, the 214th anniversary of the abolition.

Acting upon the advice of the criminologist Cesare Beccaria, Pietro Leopoldo I of Tuscany signed a decree abolishing the death penalty and torture on 30 November 1786, making Tuscany the first country to do so. Reintroduced in 1790 for the crime of insurrection against the state, the penalty would later (29 August 1817) be further extended by Grand Duke Ferdinand III to cover crimes against common law (see Montepescali, page 282). However, that decision was made during the period of reactionary restoration that followed the fall of Napoleon and the Congress of Vienna. In 1859 the provisional government of Tuscany would abolish the death penalty for good. The kingdom of Italy later adopted the abolition in 1889, with a nearly unanimous vote by the two elected chambers of parliament, but in fact the penalty had not been used since the general amnesty decreed by Umberto I of Savoia on 18 January 1878. Executions, however, were still permitted under the military penal code and the death penalty continued to be applied in the Italian colonies. In 1926 the Fascist government reintroduced the death penalty for attempts on the life of members of the royal family or the head of state, as well as for crimes against national security. The Constitution of the Italian Republic voted on 27 December 1947 would then finally abolish the death penalty... in peace time. It remained part of the military penal code until 1994.

THE CORONATION OF THE VIRGIN ⑥

A forgotten masterpiece

Church of San Pietro in Badia a Roti
Open during Sunday mass, 10.00-11.15
Otherwise, phone: Camilla Sawicki on 338 592 99 12; Claudio Bressan on
339 244 70 23; or Andrea Agresti on 340 543 61 69

Hidden away in the Tuscan countryside, to the south-east of Chianti, the church of San Pietro in Badia contains a small masterpiece, unknown even to many of the local residents.

Painted in 1472 by Neri di Bicci (1419-1491), this Coronation of the Virgin stands just behind the high altar. Perfectly lit, it is guaranteed to take your breath away when you enter the church. The decorative richness, dazzling palette, and gilt background of the work make this painting a gem which you definitely must not miss if you are in the neighbourhood. Note also its unusual ring of angels around the Virgin.

Commissioned for the church in 1471 by the local parish priest, Father Bartolomeo, the painting was on loan to Florence in the years 1862-1913: the church was undergoing restoration and it was feared the painting might be damaged. The somewhat less successful lunette above the picture depicts The Annunciation.

Built in the 12th century, the church itself was originally part of an abbey, which is now undergoing restoration. Unusually, it is not aligned east-west, which suggests it was built on the site of an earlier structure that dated from pre-Christian times.

PARCO ARTISTICO BUM BUM GÀ

Modern art in the middle of the Tuscan countryside

Borrolungo District, Via Ossaia - 52025 Montevarchi (AR)
Sculptor: Carmelo Librizzi
E-Mail : librizzi3@librizzicarmelo.191.it
Tel: 055 91 02 157 - 329 98 18 574
Opening hours: daily 9.00-18.00
Free admission
Directions: the Borrolungo district which is the site of the Parco Artistico Bum
Bum Gà stands about one kilometre from the village, on the other side of the
railway track. The way is indicated by various signposts which lead you onto a
narrow earthen track. Don't worry: just when you think you have gone the wrong
way, you are practically there.

Created from 1976 onwards by the sculptor and musician Carmelo Librizzi, this Art Park can be visited as an open-air exhibition of works laid out in the beautiful countryside of the Valdarno. However, when you look more closely, you see that there is nothing casual about the way the artist has organised the works. The park is, in effect, a reflection upon the modern art of its day (it was started in the 1970s) and upon how art might develop in the future. Its name is taken from that of the isolated Australian village which is the setting of Luigi Zampa's 1971 film Bello Onesto Emigrato Australia sposerebbe compaesana illibata (Good-looking and honest emigrant to Australia looking for

a virgin from his home town with a view to marriage), which starred Alberta Sordi as an Italian provincial rather ill-at-ease in his new world.

Though you might not entirely understand what the park's creator is trying to communicate, a visit to the place is both unusual and pleasant; the location itself is splendid, partly because it is nothing like the typical setting for a display of modern art.

In summer, Carmelo Librizzi organises shows, concerts and events, at which the children from the schools of Montevarchi are more likely to be participants than mere spectators.

THE GOLDEN TREE IN THE
MUNICIPAL MUSEUM OF LUCIGNANO

A Golden Tree that brings good luck to lovers

22, Piazza del Tribunale - 52046 Lucignano (AR)
Tel: 0575 83 68 99
E-Mail: lucignano@comune.lucignano.ar.it
http://www.comune.lucignano.ar.it
Opening hours: in winter, Tuesday, Thursday and Friday 10.00-13.00 and 14.30-
17.30, Saturday and Sunday 10.00-13.00 and 14.30-18.00; in summer: Tuesday,
Wednesday, Thursday, Saturday and Sunday 10.00-13.00 and 14.30-18.00
Closed on Mondays
Admission: 3 €, reduced: 2 €

An exceptional example of the skill of Arezzo's goldsmiths, this Golden Tree has no equal anywhere in the world and is the pride of the Lucignano Municipal Museum. Also known as the "Tree of Life," the "Tree of Lucignano," the "Tree of Love," or the "Tree of St. Francis," this Golden Tree is, in fact, a reliquary.

Standing 2.6 m high and made of silver and gilded copper, it was created over the period 1350 to 1471. Ugolino da Vieri and Gabriello d'Antonio are both mentioned as having played a part in its making.

The tree consists of a trunk and twelve branches. At the top is a crucifix and a pelican; the bird was supposed to peck its breast in order to feed its young with its own blood, and thus became a symbol of Christ's sacrifice on the Cross. On the branches – six to each side – are golden leaves, miniatures, enamels, medallions adorned with rock crystal and coral (the latter's colour recalling that of Christ's blood) and small reliquaries that once held fragments of the True Cross (now empty).

The tree was stolen on 28 September 1914. Three years later it was found hidden in a cave outside the village of Sarterano (near Siena), about 60 kilometres to the south of here; however, some of its enamel works and coral pieces were missing; originally there were 72. The name "Tree of Love" comes from the fact that the tree is supposed to bring good luck to the newly-weds – and renewed sexual vigour to the elderly couples – who place flowers or petals at its base.

NEARBY
The Triumph of Death ⑨
Church of San Francesco. Piazza San Francesco - 52046 Lucignano (AR)
Built in the 13th century, the church of San Francesco contains a very striking fresco by Bartolo di Fredi (1330-1410), which has recently undergone painstaking restoration. This depicts The Triumph of Death with the sort of breath-taking realism that one more readily associates with a modern film poster. In a programme broadcast on RAI3 in 2006, Philippe Daverio described the work as the "first 'period' example of 'comic book art.'"

ROMAN MOSAIC IN THE DE MUNARI CHEMIST'S SHOP

Mosaics to order

82, Corso Matteoti
53041 Asciano (SI)
Tel : 0577 71 81 24
Visits: apply to the chemist. No more than two people at a time. Groups not admitted
Shop opening hours: 9.00-13.00 and 15.30-19.30, Saturday 9.00-13.00

A large area of the floor in the back shop of the De Munari pharmacy (formerly Francini Naldi) is part of a Roman mosaic that is said to date from the 1st century AD.

To see this amazing hidden gem, you have to go through the labyrinthine storage area behind the main shop and then descend into the basement. Covering a total of 180 m2, the sumptuous underground pavement was discovered in 1889. The richness and refinement of the mosaic suggested that it was part of thermal baths fed by the sulphurous waters of the Bestina torrent. However, studies by some archaeologists seem to support the notion that it belonged to a villa built by Domitius Afrus, a famous orator from in Nimes in Gaul who served the emperor Caligula (12-41 AD). It is said that afterwards the villa became the property of Domitia Lucilla, the mother of the emperor Marcus Aurelius (121-180 AD).

> The chemist is kind enough to allow the curious to see this marvellous feature of his premises. Do not ask to see it when the shop is full or turn up just before closing time. Note: the mosaics were being repaired during my last visit, and this work may still be underwayso perhaps they are still undergoing repair.

THE ARBORARIO OF
THE VINEYARD OF THE ARTISTS

A place where wine meets art

NostraVita Vineyard in an area known as Nostra Signora della Vita 229B
Montalcino (Province of Siena)
Tel: 0577-848-487 or 329-4423163
Email: info@nostravita.it - www.nostravita.it

In the Consorzio Brunello di Mondalcino's list of wine producers, the NostraVita cellar seems barely more than just one of a number of smaller less well-qualified cellars — certainly an excellent wine, but with no really special qualities.

However, visit this cellar and you will definitely discover a wine of the highest quality. Yet the wine almost takes a back seat when you become aware of the creativity and aestheticism in the family that produces it; and of the artistic projects and even the philosophy of life that motivate them.

The members of this family don't like to say that they are proprietors of a vineyard; they would rather talk about their (roughly) 10,000 vine stocks. This focus on the plants themselves helps us to understand the kind of special respect they have in relation to their estate.

Indeed, they adorn their vineyard with sculptures, some crafted by themselves, others by international artists, following the tenet that art always interacts with nature — and vice versa, since they also have a tree growing in the living room of their house.

But the ultimate meeting place of nature and art, so important for this family, is the *arborario*, a word derived from *arbore* (tree) and *erbario* (herbarium). In short it can be described as a "tree of trees". Put simply, it is a collection of wooden 'books', each dedicated to a tree and a piece of wood from the tree it represents. Inside each are contained its pollen, leaves, resins, and parasites, as well as a monograph and other related information.

These books, created by the vineyard owner Annibale Parisi in collaboration with his naturalist friend Mario Morellini, are arranged on shelving (itself structured in the form of a tree for special effect) in a room that also contains an extensive collection of books on the history of the Val d'Orcia. A collection of pipes made from tree heath (*erica arborea*), also created by Annibale Parisi, is also on display.

But let's not forget about the wine! Every bottle from Brunello di Montalcino comes with a hand painted label to certify the wine's unique character. Tastings are free and are intended as a way of thanking nature, as opposed to being merely the commercial promotion of a product. Everyone who is drawn to the idea of the union of art and nature, and would like to make a contribution to it, is welcome here.

THE GIANT SUNDIAL OF PIENZA ⑫

An astonishing astronomical phenomenon only occurring twice each year

Cathedral of Santa Maria Assunta
Piazza Pio II
53026 Pienza (SI)

The cathedral of Santa Maria Assunta was inaugurated on 29 August 1462. It is remarkable because twice each year the shadow which falls within the nine paving slabs of the area alongside it is exactly the same size as the building itself. A ring carved into the stone corresponds perfectly with the oculus of the cathedral, demonstrating that the correspondence is no matter of chance.

The cathedral was the work of the architect Bernardo Rossellino and was commissioned by Pope Pius II, a native of this town (which later took its name from this famous son). Probably the pontiff wanted an edifice that would make a real impact upon the local population and this is why the architect gave the cathedral a north-south – rather than the usual east-west – alignment. This meant that twice a year the remarkable phenomenon occurred: ten or eleven days after the Spring equinox (on 1 April) and ten or eleven days before the Autumn equinox (on 11 September). The effect was calculated to occur at solar noon, which means one must now allow for the difference between summer and winter time and the gap in minutes between local time as reckoned in the 15th century and current 21st century standard time.

It should be noted that an approximate version of the phenomenon occurs in the days preceding and following the above dates, given that the building's shadow only shifts some 15cm a day.

The extraordinary feature of this cathedral-sundial was only recently rediscovered, thanks to the architect Jan Pieper. To know more, see his *Pienza. Il Progetto di una Visione Umanistica del Mondo*, published by *Edizioni Menges* in 2000.

The Julian calendar: why did saint Teresa of Avila die on the night between 4 and 15 october 1582...?

The Julian calendar – which owes its name to the fact it was instituted during the reign of Julius Caesar – remained in force until the year 1582, when Pope Gregory XIII introduced what became known as the Gregorian calendar.

This reform largely concerned the question of leap years; the previous system had resulted in the calendar date lagging behind the actual annual cycle. The most spectacular effect of the introduction of the new calendar was the suppression of ten days in the year 1582.

That is why St. Teresa of Avila died on the night between 4 and 15 October 1582...

The "Earthly Paradise" of Pienza

About 50 km from Siena, the magnificent small town of Pienza, whose historic centre was listed as a UNESCO World Heritage site in 1996, is one of the very few ideal Renaissance city projects to come to fruition. Before 1462, Pienza was just a village called Corsignano, blighted by long periods of feudal wars. Back in his birthplace during a trip to Mantua, Pope Pius II (Enea Silvio Piccolomini, 1405-1464) decided in 1459, the year after he was elected pope, to raise a city that would express the Earthly Paradise. He chose his home village of Corsignano. To transform the village into a true Utopia as well as a replica of the City of God described by St. Augustine, Pius II bestowed his papal name, meaning "pure", on Pienza. He had the "pure city" built in just over three years with the aid of the sculptor, architect and town planner Bernardo di Matteo Gamberelli, known as Rossellino (1409-1464), a pupil of the famous Leon Battista Alberti (1404-1472).

Thus on 29 August 1462, for the feast of St. John the Baptist, Pius II dedicated the cathedral to St. Mary and inaugurated the new town of Pienza.

Pius II was a great humanist and man of letters. He wrote two literary works which became the first papal autobiography: *La criside* and *La storia di due amanti* (The Story of Two Lovers). In the latter, he reveals himself to be an avid follower of the lay order *La Fede Santa* (The Sacred Faith) and the group of poets *Fideli d'Amore* (Faithful of Love), and made Dante Alighieri the mentor of his ideal of Love. In these works, Divine Love was celebrated at *Locus Amoenus*, a sort of Earthly Paradise inhabited by men and women endowed with Wisdom (symbolised by the planet Uranus) and Love (symbolised by

the planet Venus). But love is mortal and passionate, and the sensual fantasies favoured by Neptune, according to the ancient astrologers, lead towards morbid vices. The Initiation of Love consists in turning fantasy into imagination and sin into virtue, which can only happen in a new location, the pure and virginal Pienza.

The strongest evidence that Pienza is a "city of Utopia" lies in the mural fresco over Porta al Murello, the main gate. It shows two angels holding a Sun above Piazza Pio II, along with the evocation to the Virgin, so that she always protects Pienza which is dedicated to her. At the summit, the dove of the Holy Spirit responds to the invocation and confirms that the town is one of Love, the principal quality of the Holy Spirit embodied by the Virgin Mary, and privileged within the context of the medieval thought of the troubadours – one of whose most famous members was Dante Alighieri. Significantly, the poet is honoured in Pienza, where a square bears his name. The town is seen as a synonym for Wisdom and Spiritual Enlightenment represented by the Ideal Woman, in this case, the Virgin herself.

In the middle of the façade of the entrance to the parish church (7th century) of the former Corsignano, where Pius II was baptised in 1405, is a relief showing a man grasping a serpent in each hand: this is the mythical representation of Christ dominating the masculine and feminine forces of the Universe. To his left, a man with a mermaid's tail struggles with a reptile: the man expresses the struggle between Ideal Love and animal passion, which is why he is half-human; while the reptile represents base instincts trying to devour his head, i.e. dominate his mind and from there to pervert the rest of his senses. It represents the initiatory struggle between the profane and the divine state.

Opposite, a man raises one hand to protect his companion, the representation of the soul, and with the other strangles a reptile, the carrier of base instincts. This is the representation of the ideal of Christian life that seeks to identify itself with the immortal soul by dominating its bodily urges: the Path to Enlightenment.

The lateral friezes in the church portico, decorated with allegories of knights and animals – mainly lions and horses – refer to the spiritual Chivalry where the horse represents Tradition and the lion the Enlightenment to be conquered. Only afterwards can you cross, literally and spiritually, Porta al Ciglio and head towards the Romitorio di Pienza (about 4 km from the historic town centre), an ancient underground tomb of Christian hermits who were dedicated to the cult of the Virgin Mary evoked as the Madonna del Latte (Madonna of the Milk). In the grotto is a statue of the Madonna endowed with six fingers, signifying that she has full possession of the sixth sense, that of Intuition and Spiritual Intelligence.

THE HISTORIC WINE CELLARS OF THE PALAZZO CONTUCCI

A cellar that has been productive for more than a thousand years

Via del Teatro, 1
Montepulciano (Province of Siena)
Open: Historic cellars open daily 9:30am—12:30pm and 2:30pm—6:30pm
At harvest time the areas where the grapes are brought are open to the public
Tel: 0578-757-006
Email: info@contucci.it
www.contucci.it

O f all the families who traditionally produced the *Vino dei Nobili* (wine of the nobles), known today as Nobile de Montepulciano, the Contucci family is the most ancient and the last to remain in residence at Montepulciano. It is recorded that the Contucci have been making grapes into wine there since 1008, a tradition carried on without interruption over forty generations. They boast that their wine is produced at the vineyard, a concept that is technically at odds with how wine is produced in cellars. Nonetheless, the cellars at the Palazzo Contucci are no less spectacular or important.

From start to finish, from the harvesting of the grapes for fermentation, the *passerillage* (a process to concentrate the sugar in the grapes for the production of *vin santo*), right through to the stage of maturing in barrels prior to bottling, the winemaking process has taken place in the same rooms for centuries. These rooms are situated deep inside a 301 metre-long building whose construction started in the year 1000 so as to form an integral part of the oldest walls of the battlements of Montepulciano.

Access is tricky nowadays because of the many slopes, twists and turns and passageways. But that was not the case at the time they were built, before the modern areas of this very beautiful medieval town existed; the town has since spread out as far as the base of the fortress.

Paradoxically, the cellars are now in the higher levels of the town, demonstrating just how ancient they are. Visits to these vaulted rooms filled with barrels of excellent wine are free of charge every day, as is the tasting of the wines produced here (a red wine, a Nobile di Montepulciano, a white wine and a *vin santo*). Some barrels are located in the former guardroom dungeons that occupied part of the ground floor of the building.

At harvest time, these underground rooms (where the grapes are brought to be fermented) are also open to the public. Though once the winemaking begins, visits are discontinued due to the carbon dioxide naturally released by the process.

ARCHAEOLOGICAL PARK OF RADICOFANI FORT

*Incredible triple pentagonal fortifications and
an Italian Robin Hood*

Open: Daily 9am—8pm. Night time visits in summer until 2am
Entry fee: 4€
Tel: 333-8388541
Email: postmaster@fortezzadiradicofani.it
www.fortezzadiradicofani.it

Strategically located on an extinct volcano, at a height of over 900 metres, on the border between the Papal States and Tuscany, along the Via Francigena, the Fortress of Radicofani was built as a look out that was meant to be seen. On a clear day it can be seen from more than 200 kilometres away and you can enjoy a 360° view of the horizon the same distance away from its watchtowers.

Founded in the 10th century by the Carolingians, it gradually increased in size until the spectacular triple pentagonal fortifications we see today were added on the initiative of the Medicis after the definitive capture of the Republic of Siena. The extremely sturdy bastions were devised at several different periods reflecting the changing requirements of the day, whether the purpose was defensive or offensive. Starting with typically medieval arrowslits, they progress to the much larger openings of the third set of ramparts, which were more advantageous for the firepower of catapults.

This fine fortress never really had to defend itself, as it always appeared impregnable from the outside, even at a distance. In fact, it has only suffered one small piece of damage during the course of its history. One of its towers was destroyed by a soldier who, on being refused promotion, committed suicide by blowing up the gunpowder magazine housed within.

However, the place was once conquered and occupied. On Christmas night in 1297, a small independent army, fleeing from the *pax guelfa* which had recently been concluded, took advantage of a lapse in concentration by the fortress's Papal guards and seized it. (Thinking they were living in times of peace, the Papal soldiers had not known about this army of political exiles!)

The chief of the exiles was Ghino di Tacco. The fortress turned into a small 'state' where Ghino's law held sway. Ghino was considered a gentleman thief: he would strip merchants of their possessions, leaving them whatever they needed to carry on with their activities; he would seize horses from noblemen passing though, but he allowed them to continue on their way on mules. Behaving in this way he 'levelled' off the social classes while protecting his companions and the peasants of the region.

Ghino's illegal confinement of the Abbot of Cluny had an outcome that was curious to say the least. The abbot was on his way to San Casciano to have treatment for his gout. As he declined to pay the tax that Ghino demanded from him as he passed the fortress, he was confined to a cell, which can still be visited today. The abbot was placed on a strict regime that did him so much good that the monk made representations on behalf of the brigand to the pope in Rome, and even had him nominated as a Knight of St. John and 'brother' of the Hospital of the Holy Spirit.

THE SECRETS OF THE ROMANTIC WOODS OF RADICOFANI

The perfect spot for Masonic symbolism enthusiasts

Access from Via Odoardo Luchini and Via Dante Alighieri
Radicofani

A Garibaldi supporter and senator in the days of the kingdom of Italy, Odoardo Luchini (1844-1906) wished to dedicate a wooded garden to his wife Isabella, a well-known painter belonging to the Macchiaioli group of artists. He decided that the perfect place to fulfil this dream was a sloping strip of land between the town walls and the fields in an area that was used as a spur road.

The wood was skilfully designed, in such a way that any manmade alterations to it would not have an adverse affect on the surrounding nature. Clearings and pleasant viewing areas were established; boulders found at the site were exposed to create features in the wood; springs were left to flow in their natural state. No excavation or levelling of the land whatsoever was allowed. Etruscan ruins unearthed by chance were treated with great respect, as were the remains of the fortress of Radicofani, which was destroyed during the Medicis' final siege in 1555. The Luchinis were freemasons, and although Odoardo was not considered to be a fully participating mason, having somehow distanced himself from the lodge, he did not shy away from openly displaying symbols of his association when he created the wood. Indeed, he turned it into a veritable path through the fraternity's initiation and secrets.

Much of what at first looks like the work of nature has in fact been carefully planned: certain trees have been planted in threes; a jar buried near the esplanade symbolises the priests' ablution basin in the Temple of Solomon; two great boulders at the start of the path leading to the pyramid symbolise Jakin and Boaz, the two bronze pillars of the Temple of Solomon; the box tree hedge, circular in shape, symbolises the all-seeing eye of God; and the large pyramid itself, with its triangular base clearly visible — these images are all associated with freemasonry.

Notice also how the colours of the stone and the vegetation blend together. Human work should always respect nature, but that does not mean that man cannot work within its framework.

Today, the woods are more or less in a state of neglect, despite the fact that members of the Grand Orient of Italy still meet at Radicofani once a year. This ceremony commences at the wood's pyramid. A public meeting is held, during which, lectures are organised and book presentations and discussions take place in the municipal theatre. Whatever their rank, members of the secret organisation are happy to answer questions from the public.

Pisa

THE JEWISH CEMETERY OF PISA

The oldest Jewish cemetery still in use in Italy

Largo Griffi Cocco, 2 - 56126 Pisa (PI)
Open: Sundays 10am-12:30pm; Wednesdays from November to May 2pm-4pm;
and from June to October 4pm-6pm. Closed during Jewish religious holidays
Admission: Guided tours by appointment (a charge applies)
Tel: 050-542-580
Email: com_ebraicapi@tin.it
www.pisaebraica.it

Situated near the Piazza dei Miracoli, next to the Monumental Cemetery, Pisa's Jewish cemetery has been in use since 1674. Although it is not the town's first Jewish graveyard, it certainly is the oldest one still in use in the whole of Italy.

Here can be found gravestones that predate the opening of the cemetery. They were brought here after the closure of burial places situated further away. Headstones here today include examples of Jewish funerary styles spanning almost every era, different styles epitomising different centuries. It's interesting to note that in Hebrew the word "cemetery" translates as "the house of life" — even though this place is intended for the dead, it is also a place for the living to remember and be with the deceased through their prayers. The little round stones placed on top the tombstones represent eternity; their smooth shape symbolises the cyclical nature of life; a flower, on the other hand, because it will soon wither, is a reminder of mortality.

Although space is becoming more limited, this cemetery is still in use. Tradition demands that the remains of the dead be buried in the ground and not be disturbed — so a new place of rest will have to be found sooner or later.

NEARBY
The Pisa Synagogue ②
Via Palestro 24 - 56126 Pisa (PI)
Visits are by appointment only at the number above or during the celebration of the Sabbath or other Jewish religious celebrations.
On the same site since it was built in 1593, the Pisa Synagogue is the town's first public one. Before that, prayers were said in private households. One of the most famous restorers, Marco Treves, gave it its present neoclassical form. As well as being the architect of the Florence Synagogue, Treves was contracted by Napoleon to carry out the restoration of the Louvre in Paris.

Already in existence in the year 859, the Jewish community in Pisa is one of the oldest in Europe along with that of Rome.

A CATHEDRAL AS A SUNDIAL

When the Pisan New Year was celebrated on 25 March

Piazza dei Miracoli - 56126 Pisa (PI)

Once a year, on 25 March, Pisa Cathedral is transformed into one immense solar clock, the light filtering through the building serving to announce the advent of the New Year. Before 1749, when the Grand Duke of Tuscany imposed 1 January as the start of the new year, it was traditional for the year to change on 25 March, which fell very close to the spring equinox. On that day the rays of the sun enter the cathedral through an oculus in the main nave and strike a plaque resting on a marble egg. This event is celebrated with a traditional procession and a brief ceremony which ends at midday with the recital of this ritual phrase: "We call upon the intercession of the Blessed Virgin Mary and of St. Ranieri, our patron saint, as, to the greater glory of God, we celebrate the year..." (the number of the Pisan year is in fact one higher than that of the usual calendar).

Reintroduced in the 1980s, this ceremony is also an act of veneration to the Virgin, to whom the cathedral is dedicated. March 25 is, in fact, the Feast of the Annunciation.

NEARBY

Amphora from the marriage feast at Cana ④

Pisa Cathedral - 56126 Pisa (PI)

To the right of the cathedral apse is a column bearing a red porphyry amphora which, according to tradition, was one of those containing the water which Jesus changed into wine at the Marriage Feast of Cana. An inscription records that the precious relic was supposedly brought back from the Holy Land after the First Crusade (1096-1099). In all of the cathedral inventories, the amphora is referred to as the "Epiphany Urn." In fact, the miracle of the changing of water into wine was traditionally believed to have taken place on the Feast of the Epiphany (January 6). One should point out that other sources say the urn dates from the 4th century AD.

Mark of the devil in Pisa Cathedral ⑤

The fifth column to your left as you walk down the nave of the cathedral from the main entrance is marked by regular series of holes forming a straight vertical line. Legend has it that these were made by the Devil, who wanted to play his own shady part in the building of the church. The story goes that, like the Devil, the holes are deceitful, for it is almost impossible to count up or down the line without getting confused and coming up with a different sum total each time (see the story concerning the bees of Ferdinando I in Florence, page 48).

Photographs courtesy of StilePisano www.stilepisano.it

THE LIZARD OF PISA CATHEDRAL \textcircled{6}

A lizard that traditionally brings good luck

Piazza del Duomo - 56126 Pisa (PI)
www.opapisa.it

The three bronze doors on the façade of Pisa Cathedral were created in the workshops of Giambologna. They depict scenes from the lives of the Christ and the Virgin Mary. Amongst the many decorative features adorning the doors, you will notice a variety of animals, including a stag, an eagle, a pelican, a dog, a frog and, on the middle door, a two-tailed lizard. Although lizards can have a wide range of symbolic meanings, popular tradition has it that this particular lizard brings good luck to those who touch it. That becomes all the more obvious when you observe the shiny gold surface of the lizard, polished smooth by people perpetually touching it. It has become a rite passed down through successive generations of high school students and undergraduates of the University of Pisa as exam time approaches. So much so that the cathedral administration recently made a decision to curtail access to the door in order to protect the reptile.

The magical properties of this lizard arise from its double-pointed tail. Doubling of things in nature has been interpreted by man either as a portent of bad luck and hardship, or conversely of good luck and abundance. If this duplication is applied to something positive, it is a portent of bad luck but when applied to something negative or of lesser value — in this case a tiny and inoffensive lizard — it brings abundance and good luck.

The cathedral's rhino

On the left door of Pisa Cathedral another curious animal can be seen: a thick-plated rhinoceros. Some have compared it to Albrecht Dürer's famous woodcut of 1515, which portrays a rhino that was brought to the West around then, the first specimen of its kind since Roman times.

The rhino had been captured in India and taken by ship to Lisbon on its way ultimately to be gifted to Pope Leo X in Rome. From Lisbon it was loaded aboard a ship bound for Latium, but on the way made a stopover in Marseille to give King François I an opportunity to view this marvellous beast. After a delay of some

weeks, the journey continued and the rhino was finally loaded onto a small craft heading for Italy. Alas, it was not long before the boat sank… but the pope did indeed receive his gift — although not before the taxidermist had done his work on it!

NEARBY

Wind rose in Piazza dei Miracoli   ⑦

Piazza dei Miracoli - 56126 Pisa (PI)

Above the roof of the ticket office in Piazza dei Miracoli is an elegant wind rose surmounted by an arch and a capital. It gives the direction of the prevailing winds. From the top clockwise, the main winds in the Mediterranean are indicated as follows (winds are named after the direction from which they blow):

Mezz: the mezzogiorno or *ostro*, the south wind
Libe: the *libeccio*, the south-west wind
Pon: the *ponente*, the west wind

Maes: the *maestrale*, the north-west wind
Tram: the *tramontana*, the north wind
Grec: the *grecale*, the north-east wind
Lev: the *levante*, the east wind
Scir: the *scirocco*, the south-east wind

On the pediment of the charterhouse at Calci near Pisa an identical rose wind is positioned rather differently: the east is shown at the top, in accordance with the medieval custom of placing the direction of Jerusalem above all others.

RELIC OF THE CROWN OF THORNS ⑧ IN THE CHURCH OF SANTA CHIARA

Still green...!

Church of Santa Chiara dall'Opera dell'Ospedale. 67, Via Roma - 56126 Pisa (PI)
The church of Santa Chiara is actually located within the Santa Chiara hospital complex (Azienda Ospedaliera Pisana), at the end of Via Roma, a short walk from Piazza dei Miracoli.

ontrary to what one would expect, the precious relic of Christ's
Crown of Thorns that gives its name to Santa Maria della Spina
[*spina* = thorn] is no longer within that church. In fact, Santa Maria
della Spina originally stood on the banks of the Arno but - in order
to protect it from flooding - in 1871 it was dismantled stone by stone
and then rebuilt on its present site. During this "removal," the relic of
Christ's Crown of Thorns was moved to Santa Chiara and has stayed
there ever since; the tabernacle for the relic which Stagio Stani created in
1534 for the church of Santa Maria della Spina stands empty.

The relic comprises a twisted section of thorn with one long prickle
and two smaller ones. It is said to have been brought to the city by a
Pisan merchant in 1266 and then presented to the Oratory of Santa
Maria al Ponte Novo in 1333. Whilst the famous Crown of Thorns
itself was bought by the sainted French King Louis IX in 1239 (see
below), it would seem that over the course of the centuries a certain
number of thorns were removed from it and presented to various cities
as exceptional tokens of gratitude. Thus, Pisa, Rome, Vicenza, and
Vasto all received a part of the famous relic.

The crown of thorns

After the Holy Shroud of Turin, the Crown of Thorns is considered
the most important relic of Christ's Passion. The first reference to
the survival of the relic dates from 409, when St. Paulinus of Nola
mentions it amongst the relics to be found in the Basilica of Mount
Zion in Jerusalem. Moved to Byzantium in order to prevent it falling
into the hands of the Persians, the Crown of Thorns was subsequently
sold to the Venetians in 1238 by the Latin emperor Baudouin de
Courtenay, whose Crusader realm was facing serious economic
difficulties. St. Louis (1215-1270) bought in 1239 and then had a
befitting reliquary built to house it: the Sainte Chapelle in Paris (some
of the stained glass windows in the church record this event). After
the French Revolution, the relics were entrusted to the canons of the
Chapter of Notre-Dame in Paris, and they are still to be found in that
cathedral, where the Crown of Thorns is put on display for the faithful
once a year (see *Secret Paris* by the same publisher).

The authenticity of such relics is, of course, difficult to establish.
However, on the one known occasion when the present reliquary was
opened (1940), it was discovered that the leaves had dried but the
ring of plaited thorns was still green!

OLD FOUNDLINGS HOSPITAL

Where children could be abandoned discreetly

Library and Documentary Archive of the Pisan Hospitals
108, Via Santa Maria - 56126 Pisa (PI)
Opening hours: Monday to Thursday 8.00-13.00 and 15.00-17.00, Friday
8.00-13.00
56 and 60, Via Santa Maria
12, Via dell'Occhio

Just a short walk from Piazza dei Miracoli is the old Foundlings Hospital. Right above the doorway is a touching reminder of the building's past: a sculpture of a baby wrapped in swaddling. In fact, right up to 1921 it was possible to abandon unwanted infants here...

The process was facilitated by something called a "wheel," a sort of rotating cradle: the infant was placed on the outside section and then the table was rotated so that, no questions asked, it was moved inside. The contraption still exists, only now it is inside the building: just push open the door at the opening times given above and you can see it.

There are similar haut-reliefs elsewhere in the city indicating other places that received abandoned children – for example, at numbers 56 and 60 Via Santa Maria, which were once 9 and 10 of the old Via Santa Maria de Ponte Novo, a street which used to ran down to the Ponte Novo (this bridge over the Arno was destroyed in the 19th century). Another, rather crude, depiction of an infant can be seen set into the wall of no. 12 Via dell'Occhio.

The foundlings' wheel

It is said that in 787, Dateus, a priest in Milan, began placing a large basket outside his church so that abandoned infants could be left there.

More organised initiatives for the reception of abandoned children were begun by the Hospice des Chanoines in Marseilles from 1188 onwards, with Pope Innocent III (1198-1216) later giving the practice the Church's benediction; he had been horrified by the terrible sight of the bodies of abandoned infants floating in the Tiber and was determined to do something to save them.

So the doors of convents were equipped with a sort of rotating cradle which made it possible for parents to leave their infant anonymously and without exposing them to the elements.

The infant was left in the outside section of the cradle, and then the parent rang a bell so that the nuns could activate the mechanism and bring the child inside. Access to the "turntable" was, however, protected by a grill so narrow that only newborn infants would fit through...

Abandoned during the 19th century, the system has, over the last twenty years, had to be re-adopted at various places in Europe due to the sharp upturn in the number of infants abandoned.

Why is the cross of the Order of Santo Stefano so similar to the Maltese Cross?

For the laymen there is very little difference between the Cross of the Military Order of Santo Stefano and the more famous Cross of the Knights of Malta. The two colours – red and white – are the opposite way round, but the form of the cross is identical. Founded in 1561, the Military Order of Santo Stefano was intended to promote the Christian faith, defend the Mediterranean against pirates, and free Christian slaves. It first fought alongside the Order of St. John of Jerusalem in the defence of Malta, the island which would give the latter order its more familiar title. As a symbol of the bond between them, the knights of Santo Stefano took the same cross as their symbol; however, like the Knights Templar (who had disappeared from western history in 1307), they chose the colour of the blood of Christ for the cross itself. Founded in 11th century Jerusalem by merchants from Amalfi (near Naples), the Sovereign Order of the Knights Hospitaller of St. John of Jeruslam (the future Knights of Malta) first took as their symbol that of the port of Amalfi, merely dropping the blue background. Then, in 1130, Raymond de Puy transformed the charitable brotherhood into a military Order and obtained from Pope Innocent II the right to a white cruciform emblem; the colour was chosen to avoid confusion with the red cross of the Templars. Shortly after being driven off the island of Rhodes by the Turks in 1523, the Order would settle on Malta. At that point, the red flag of the island – inherited from the period when it had been occupied by the Normans – became the background to the white cross. And thus the Maltese Cross came about.

The meaning of the eight points in the Maltese Cross and the cross of the Order of Santo Stefano

The eight points in the Maltese Cross signify various things:

- The eight nationalities of the original knights of the Order of St. John of Jerusalem (the future Order of Malta) or the eight principles they undertook to live by: spirituality, simplicity, humility, compassion, justice, pity, sincerity and patience.

- The eight virtues which a knight of the Order of Malta was expected to possess: loyalty, pity, frankness, courage, honour, contempt of death, solidarity with the sick and poor, respect for the Catholic Church.

- The Eight Beatitudes which Christ listed in his Sermon on the Mount (St. Matthew's Gospel, Chapter 5):

Blessed are the poor in spirit: for theirs is the kingdom of heaven. (Verse 3)

Blessed are the meek: for they shall posses the land. (Verse 4)

Blessed are they who mourn: for they shall be comforted. (Verse 5)

Blessed are they that hunger and thirst after justice: for they shall have their fill. (Verse 6)

Blessed are the merciful: for they shall obtain mercy. (Verse 7)

Blessed are the clean of heart: for they shall see God. (Verse 8)

Blessed are the peacemakers: for they shall be called the children of God. (Verse 9)

Blessed are they that suffer persecution for justice' sake, for theirs is the kingdom of heaven. (Verse 10)

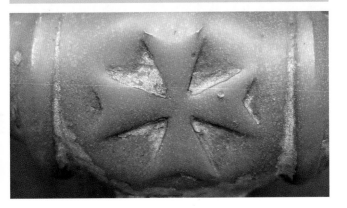

THE MUSSOLINI PORTRAIT IN THE CHURCH OF SAN FRANCESCO

Mussolini in stained glass in a 14th century church

Piazza San Francesco - 56127 Pisa (PI)

In the 1930s Francesco Mossmeyer was commissioned to carry out restoration work on the church of San Francesco. He produced new stained glass windows for the left side of the nave. Naturally these depict episodes from the lives of the saints… but there is also a figure who bears a striking resemblance to Benito Mussolini. The windows were produced when Il Duce ruled supreme in Italy, so some have argued that this similarity is far from being an accident…

Another souvenir from the Mussolini era

From the top of the famous Leaning Tower, looking towards the Baptistery, one can see a rather curiously-shaped building directly outside the city walls. This Istituto Technico Industriale was built during the period of Fascism and its M-shaped design was clearly intended as a homage to Mussolini

Why Saint-Tropez owes its name to a Pisan knight...

In the year 68 AD, the Roman emperor Nero was present at a ceremony in the Temple of Diana at Pisa and claimed "Diana is mistress of the world." Torpè, a convert to Christianity, dared to contradict him: "You are mistaken, Nero. There is only one master; and that master is God!"

Upon leaving Pisa, Nero asked a certain Satellicus to make sure, by whatever means necessary, that Torpè abjured his faith. Tied to a column, Torpè was flogged; but at the very first strokes, the column collapsed on the torturers and upon the said Satellicus. Then the Christian was stretched out on the wheel, but that, too, broke. Then he was thrown to savage beasts, but they apparently had no appetite for him. Eventually he was beheaded and his body – together with a cockerel and a dog – was put in a skiff and pushed out into the Arno.

As you might have gathered, this boat finally ran aground at Saint-Tropez, which took Torpè as its patron saint.

Cogolin, a nearby village, takes its name from the coq on the boat, and Grimaud, another nearby village, from its canine companion (grimaud in Old French meant "dog").

The church of San Torpè.

20, Via Carlo Fedeli.

Open weekdays 9.00-12.00 and 15.45-17.30, Sunday and holidays 15.45- 17.30.

THE LAST PILLORY RING IN PIAZZA CAIROLI

Where thieves and other wrongdoers were exposed to public derision

Piazza Cairoli - 56127 Pisa (PI)

The thick metal ring at the base of a column in Piazza Cairoli (the one furthest from the river) is a reminder of much crueller days.

It was here that criminals and wrongdoers were chained for public pillory; in fact the square used to be called Piazza della Berlina (*berlina* = pillory).

Here, the criminals sentenced to this form of punishment (lasting anything from a few hours to a few days) were left at the mercy of public wrath and derision: they could be insulted, spat upon and even hit.

Pillories would be abolished throughout Italy at the end of the 18th century; in Tuscany they came to an end with the abolition of torture (and capital punishment) in 1786.

NEARBY ⑫
An old-style weights and measures conversion table
15, Piazza delle Vettovaglie
56127 Pisa (PI)

On 28 July 1861 Italy replaced the old units of weight and measure – which could vary from region to region – with the new metric system. It took time for people to learn and accept the new measures, and in the interim conversion tables were displayed in towns and villages

throughout the country - primarily in the marketplace or on the main street where market gardeners set up their stalls.

In Pisa, one of these conversion tables can still be seen at number 15 in Piazza Vettovaglie, the old marketplace. To the right of this table, a glass panel in the ground gives you a view down into one of the city's old underground grain silos.

Such conversion tables still survive in a number of other towns, including Campaglia Marittima (outside Livorno), where it can be seen in Via Roma.

PALAZZO ALLA GIORNATA

The extraordinary origin of Palazzo Alla Giornata

43/44, Lungarno Antonio Pacinotti - 56127 Pisa (PI)

Located on the banks of the Arno, Palazzo alla Giornata (meaning "by the day") was built in the 17th century and currently houses the offices of the Chancellor of Pisa University. A bronze plaque on the pediment of the façade is engraved with the name of the palazzo; underneath – at the level of the keystone of the vault – hang three chain links.

Various theories have been put forward with regard to the name and the symbolic significance of the chain. In his *Dizionario Geografico Fisico della Toscana*, Emanuele Repetti admits to being unable to solve the enigma, but does mention that the palazzo is said to have incorporated the church of San Biago alle Catene (*catena* = chain) when it was built. The most likely theory, however, seems to be the following.

In the 17th century, the ship carrying a Pisan knight to Sardinia was boarded by Saracens. After fierce fighting, the knight was taken prisoner and carried off to Algiers, where he was entrusted to the keeping of one of the Bey's favourites. Impressed by the Pisan's courage, the favourite suggested that he should abjure his religion, "take the turban," and enter the service of the Bey. With each refusal from the Italian, his captor made the conditions of his captivity even harsher. One day, seeing that the man continued to respect the Friday fast by abstaining from meat, he mockingly promised: "The Friday when you agree to eat meat, I will give you your freedom." Some months later, the prisoner asked his gaoler for a meal of meat and rich desserts even though it was a Friday. Convinced that this meant the Pisan knight was abjuring his faith, the Arab kept his promise and restored the man's freedom, giving him as a souvenir three links of the chain he had had to wear in captivity.

What he did not know was that, that year, Christmas fell on a Friday, thus Christians were for that one day exempt from the rule of fasting.

Upon his return to Pisa, the knight had this palace built on the banks of the Arno. The three links of the chain were hung as an ex-voto just above the entrance, and the words alla Giornata were engraved on the pediment. The phrase was intended to remind people that even in the worst adversity one must maintain hope; one day is enough to bring about a complete turnaround in one's fortunes.

THE FIBONACCI SEQUENCE ON THE CHURCH OF SAN NICOLA

An homage in art to a great Pisan mathematician

Church of San Nicola
Via Santa Maria,2
56127 Pisa (PI)

If you didn't know, you would be unlikely to guess that one of the exterior lunettes of the Church of San Nicola in Pisa is actually designed on the basis of very precise mathematical rules. Evidently it was the artist's desire to incorporate Fibonacci's number sequence into the design of his work, in homage to the great Pisan mathematician who lived around the same time that the lunettes on the façade were created, between 1175 and 1235.

The hidden message in the marquetry was included for educational purposes by the artist. But it was not until it was deciphered by Professor Pietro Armienti of the University of Pisa some years ago that its message was finally revealed, and this thanks to simple geometrical observations he made.

To help understand Professor Armienti's analysis we must look at his reasoning. If you take as a basic unit the circles with the smallest diameter featured in the marquetry, the next up in size will have double the diameter, the next will follow Fibonacci's sequence whereby the rate of increase to the next size up will be the sum of the two previous increases – 1, 2, 3, 5, 8, 13, 21, 34, 55, 89, 144 — and so on to infinity.

Those circles with a diameter of five divide into quarters the small squares at the corners of the largest enclosing square in which the main circle is inscribed. The middle circle has a diameter of thirteen and the circle inscribed within the small squares a diameter of eight. Last but not least, the largest circle that inscribes the enclosing marquetry square has a diameter of 55, still following Fibonacci's sequence.

What is the Fibonacci sequence?

Designed as a mathematical representation of the growth of the rabbit population, this sequence of whole numbers is often repeated in nature. For example, the number of petals, stamens and flower clusters of many plants is practically always a number belonging to Fibonacci's sequence. The sequence produces a harmony of proportions, which is also notably present and visible in the design of many seashells and the configuration of the leaves of some trees. The sequence itself is not difficult to understand: each number is the sum of the two previous numbers: 1, 1, 2, 3, 5, 8, 13 . . . 1+0=1; 1+1=2; 1+2=3; 2+3=5, and so on.

It follows from this that the terms between one number and the next number in the sequence carry on increasing. This growth pattern can also be clearly expressed graphically. Fibonacci's spiral, which is formed by drawing circular arcs connecting the opposite corners of squares in the Fibonacci tiling, is well known.

The sequence can be represented in all sorts of complex ways using an infinite variety of interplaying shapes that come into contact with each other, just like the one produced in the lunette of the church in Pisa.

PUBLIC TOILETS OF
THE ALBERGO COBIANCHI

From luxury hotel to public convenience

Piazza XX Settembre - 56127 Pisa (PI)
Opening hours: 9.00-13.00 and 15.00-19.00
Admission: 0.50 €

At the beginning of the 20th century, the boom in tourism meant that new hotels were built in a number of Italian cities. Providing a new service to meet the needs of an increasingly urbanised lifestyle, these specialised in short-stay customers – either tourists passing through or people from the outlying areas who had to stay in town overnight. Work on this particular hotel in Pisa unearthed 700 gold coins bearing the image of the Roman emperor Augustus (for some obscure reason, only 229 are accounted for!), with the building finally being opened to the public in 1926.

The disastrous flood of 1966, when the nearby Arno burst its banks, devastated the hotel, which was not restored because changing trends had led to a sharp decline in its clientele. However, some restoration work was carried out in 1998, to convert the place into public toilets. This means the present-day visitor gets the chance to walk down the two long corridors which used to be lined with bedrooms and bathrooms. Despite the damage caused by the flood and subsequent neglect, one still gets some idea of the luxury and refinement of the original establishment, the name of whose owner, Cleopatro Cobianchi, can still be seen on the sign. Cobianchi would also set up various other short-stay hotels, most notably in Milan and Turin.

Santa Bona: the patron saint of hoteliers

Born in 1156 in a modest house of the San Martino district in Pisa, Bona would lose her father, Bernardo, when she was three years old. Her Corsican-born mother, Berta, then struggled against hardship to raise the child. When the girl was 7, she had a vision of receiving a benediction for the crucifix she was passing. This was the first of a number of visions that would lead her to dedicate herself to the religious life. When just 13, Bona set out on a pilgrimage to Jerusalem. Captured by the Saracens during her return voyage, she suffered terribly as their prisoner. Released thanks to a Pisan merchant who "bought" her, she would nevertheless not give up her calling as a pilgrim, dedicating herself to helping those who found themselves in difficulty while travelling along the dangerous pilgrimage routes of the times. She went nine times to Santiago de Compostela (a journey which took around nine months) and on numerous occasions to Rome. She would make her last pilgrimage to Santiago at the age of 48, "transported" there by the apostle himself. On 2 March 1962, Pope John XXIII declared her the patron saint of hoteliers. Thus St. Bona is much venerated by those working in the tourist trade.
Church of San Martino. 1, Piazza San Martino.

THE WELL OF SAINT UBALDESCA  ⑯

Bread into flower petals and water into wine

Church of San Sepolcro
Piazza San Sepolcro - 56127 Pisa (PI)
Mass: Saturday at 18.00

The church of San Sepolcro has a well that is associated with a remarkable 12th century miracle.

Born in Calcinia (near Pisa) around 1136, Ubaldesca Taccini would from a very early age reveal her great spirituality and charity. One day, while she was working in the fields, a stranger asked her for a piece of bread. Without hesitating, the girl ran home and filled her smock with food. From a distance, her father saw what she was doing and, when he caught up with her, forbade her to give their food to a stranger. Otherwise what would they have to eat? For the first time in her life Ubaldesca found herself forced to lie, saying that she merely had wild flowers in her smock. A miracle then took place: multicoloured petals fell from the smock, flying off in the breeze.

At 15 years of age Ubaldesca would become a nun within the Hospital of the Knights of St. John of Jerusalem (later the Knights of Malta) which had been built around the church of San Sepolcro in Pisa. Thereafter she would dedicate herself to helping pilgrims.

One day, whilst she was drawing water from the well, a group of pilgrims on their way to Rome asked her for something to drink. She raised the pail from the well, and to everyone's amazement the water had been transformed into wine…

Ubaldesca is the patron saint of Calcinia, her home town, and is venerated by the Order of Malta.

> The entrance to the church is a few steps below street level. Like many other buildings in Pisa, the church has subsided because of underground infiltration by the waters of the Arno. (See "The Other Leaning Towers" below).

The other leaning towers of Pisa

As well as the famous tower in Piazza dei Miracoli, Pisa has three other bell towers that stand at an angle to the vertical: the 12th century San Michele degli Salzi, in the Orticaria district; San Sisto, near Piazza dei Cavalieri; and San Nicola, in Via Santa Maria. Being incorporated within the surrounding buildings, the latter bell tower appears to be in no danger of falling down. It is unusual in that the base is cylindrical, with the body of the tower then becoming octagonal before ending up hexagonal.

San Sisto - Via dei Mille.
San Michele degli Scalzi - Via San Michele degli Scalzi.
San Nicola - Via Santa Maria.

STATUE OF KINZICA DE SISMONDI ⑰

Kinzica, heroine of Pisa: legend and fact

7, Via San Martino - 56127 Pisa (PI)

Via San Martino, on the left bank of the Arno, stands in an area of the city that was once called Kinzica. Here, there is a curious marble statue of an elegant Roman matron that dates from the 3rd century AD. Over time, the figure depicted became identified with the name of the district itself.

Although there are various versions of the story of how a young woman saved the inhabitants of Pisa from Saracen raiders, it does seem the story is based on real events.

In 1004-1005, or 1016 or 1024 – the date varies – the Pisan fleet was besieging Reggio Calabria in order to drive out the Saracens. But the pirates took advantage of the fact that Pisa itself had been left almost undefended and attacked the city. According to one account, Kinzica, who could not sleep that night, raised the alarm by ringing the bell in the Palazzo degli Anziani, thus awakening the people of the city and enabling them to escape… or perhaps arm themselves and drive off the Saracens… or perhaps (according to a third version) the mere sound of the bells scared off the attackers. There is even a version in which Kinzica, first to see the advancing enemy, took up arms against them and distinguished herself by her courage in battle.

Then there is her name itself: some argue it comes from Arabic (the district where the girl lived was that inhabited principally by foreigners), others that it derives from the old Lombard dialect…

One thing is certain: for the people of Pisa, Kinzica is a heroine. She is remembered with particular veneration during the annual Regatta delle Repubbliche Marittime, a boating competition between the four great maritime republics of Italy: Pisa, Venice, Amalfi and Genoa. The event is hosted by each of these four cities in turn.

Lucca

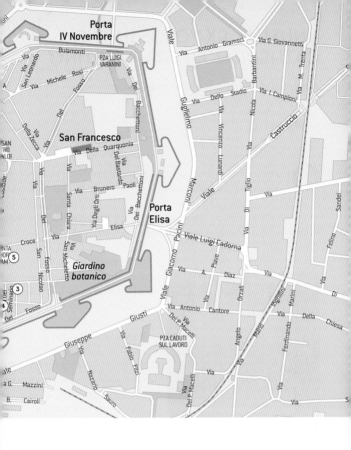

UNUSUAL EX-VOTOS IN THE CATHEDRAL OF SAN MARTINO

A metal axe that suddenly went soft

Piazza San Martino
55100 Lucca (LU)

O n a pillar just in front of the Chapel of the Holy Visage in the Cathedral of San Martino is a strange axe sticking through a thick grill. Above, a Latin inscription records a miracle that happened in 1334, when a certain Giovanni di Lorenzo from the Comté d'Arras in France tried to help a man who had been attacked in the town of Pietralunga (Umbria). The victim died of his wounds and, as they had not witnessed the attack, the townspeople assumed that the Frenchman was the murderer. Imprisoned and then sentenced to be beheaded he prayed to the Holy Visage of Lucca (see page 175) for the truth to come to light. When the executioner brought his iron axe down on Giovanni's neck, the blade suddenly went so soft that it did not even leave a mark on the skin. The miracle was repeated another two times before finally, in accordance with custom, the condemned man was set free and his innocence recognised.

An ill-lit glass case not far from this axe in the church contains a real horse's tail. This unusual trophy was offered as an ex-voto to the Holy Visage (see page 175) by Stefano Orsetti, a native of Lucca who served as the commanding officer of a cavalry regiment in the Austro-Hungarian army; he had cut the tail from the horse of an enemy during a battle against the Turks fought at Petrovaradin (Hungary).

Photos courtesy of the Cathedral of San Martino, Lucca

Why is the façade of the cathedral asymmetrical?

Curiously, the façade of San Martino cathedral in Lucca is highly asymmetrical: the right arch is much narrower than the central and left ones, an extremely rare example of "architectural licence" in a Christian building. According to popular legend, this imperfection was thought to be a sign that the cathedral was the work of the Devil. The same legend claims that the oddly rounded stone at the base of the bell tower was also diabolical, and had been cut by Lucifer himself. In fact, this cornerstone was perfectly designed by the ancient brotherhood of free builders, led by Guido da Como, whose knowledge of architecture and symbolism was such that it was taken, at a time of illiteracy and superstition, as coming from the Devil himself! The fact that the arch on the right is narrower than the others has nothing diabolical about it either; on the contrary, it is the symbolic indication of the *right way*, the narrow path of which Jesus speaks in the Bible ("Enter through the narrow gate," Matthew 7:13). The same path opens onto the salvation reached after triumphantly travelling through the initiatory maze of everyday trials. We are therefore faced with an architectural allegory of the labyrinth incorporated on the right side of the portico (see page 152).

Symbol of Spiritual Enlightenment

Also on the façade of San Martino cathedral are scenes from the martyrdom of St. Regulus, depicted in the opening above the entrance to the right-hand aisle. This saint, thought to have lived in Tuscany around 545, was martyred under the rule of Totila, king of the Ostrogoths. Here Regulus really represents much more than the Christian martyr. He is also the symbol of Regulus, the brightest star in the constellation Leo, which belongs astrologically to the Sun and is therefore also the symbol of Spiritual Enlightenment: the "regulus" is a real "little king" in so far as he has experienced spiritual awakening. The marble slab that shows the Sun beneath a crowned serpent swallowing a man evokes the same message: the Eastern treaties of primitive Hinduism refer to the electromagnetic force that circulates inside man and nature. They call it *Kundalini* and describe it as a crowned serpent that rises up while spiritually enlightening man. The serpent that swallows the man (before spewing him out again) expresses the idea that the internal nature of man is transmuted or "vomited" into his higher nature (see *Secret Milan* in this series of guidebooks). Early Christian iconography also leans towards this idea: in the biblical story of Jonah and the whale Leviathan, the act of swallowing and regurgitating someone is a common way of representing profane death and initiatory resurrection.

THE LABYRINTH IN LUCCA CATHEDRAL

A real spiritual initiation

Piazza San Martino - 55100 Lucca (LU)

Carved to the right of the main doorway into the Cathedral is a labyrinth measuring some 50 cm in diameter. The accompanying Latin inscription reads: "This is the labyrinth designed by the Cretan Daedalus. None of those who ventured into it ever found their way out, with the exception of Theseus, who did so thanks to the thread Ariadne gave him out of love." Various explanations have been put forward regarding the symbolic significance of the labyrinth (see below). This one was once the last hope of salvation for those sentenced to death. On his way to the scaffold, the condemned man was brought to the labyrinth, and if he could, at his first attempt, trace a route through it, then his life was spared.

Labyrinths

According to legend, one of the first ever labyrinths was constructed by Daedalus to contain the Minotaur, a monster born of the love of Queen Pasiphae, wife of Minos, King of Crete, for a bull. Archaeologists have argued that the elaborate ground plan of Minos's royal palace at Knossos (Crete) was the origin of this legend. Only three people were said to have found their way through this mythical labyrinth. One was Theseus, who had come to Crete to kill the monster; he was helped in his task by Ariadne, Minos's daughter, who had fallen in love with him and gave him a thread so that he could find his way back out (the famous "Ariadne's thread"). The other two were Daedalus himself and his son Icarus, after Minos had imprisoned them there. Some legends say the king was anxious that the secret of the labyrinth should never be betrayed; others claim the imprisonment was punishment for having given Ariadne the idea of the thread. The labyrinth was so perfectly designed that even Daedalus could only find his way out by flying above it, having made himself and his son wings out of feathers and wax. Designs or engravings of labyrinths are to be found in numerous ancient civilisations (Mesopotamian, Egyptian, Hopi, Navajo, etc.) and there are vestiges in Europe dating back to prehistoric times. The symbol of the labyrinth was also used by early Christianity and can be seen in the Rome catacombs, as well as Italian churches such as San Michele Maggiore (Pavia) and the cathedral in Lucca. There was also a mosaic in San Savino (Piacenza). In France there are fine examples in the cathedrals of Chartres and Rheims. Usually these are located on the western side of the church, the direction associated with demons and death because it is in the west that the sun sets. As it was believed that demons could only move in straight lines, the elaborate path of the labyrinth prevented them reaching the altar. The labyrinth is also associated with ideas regarding the course of life, reflecting the notion that Man is lost within the Universe and does not know where he comes from or where he is going. But the very centre of the labyrinth, reached after an often painful and tortuous journey of initiation, might well represent a point of divine salvation, a heavenly Jerusalem. The flight of Daedalus and Icarus to arrive at this goal

therefore symbolises the elevation of the spirit towards knowledge and of the soul towards God. Similarly, the thread with which Adriane supplies Theseus shows how the love of one person for another can provide another way out of the absurdity of the human condition.

VISIT TO THE HOUSE OF SAINT GEMMA GALGANI

A forgotten saint

Congregazione Missionaria Sorelle di S. Gemma. Casa Giannini
10, Via del Seminario - 55100 Lucca (LU)
Visits by appointment only.
Opening hours; summer, 9.00-12.30 and 15.00-19.00; winter, 9.00-12.00 and 15.00-18.00
Free admission and guided tour
Tel: 0583 48 237
E-Mail: cgianninilucca@libero.it

Venerated rather more in Spain and Chile than in Italy, St. Gemma Galgani (see below) lived in Lucca at 10, Via del Seminario. The congregation responsible for the chapel of Santa Maria della Rosa also provides visitors with an interesting and moving guided tour through her house.

The visit begins in the dining-room, which has been kept as it was at the time of the saint's death. A plaque on the table indicates where she sat at meals. The rooms are adorned with photographs and a powerfully expressive crucifix, which is contained within a cabinet that can be kept open or shut. Most astonishing of all is the photograph of the saint which reveals how exceptionally beautiful she was. The relics relating to her stigmata are particularly interesting. There are pieces of cloth from her garments that are stained with the blood that flowed from her wounds and from her crown of thorns. There is also the copy of her autobiography which the devil tried to burn…

Saint Gemma Galgani

Born on 12 March 1878 at Camigliano (outside Lucca), where her parents kept a chemist's shop, Gemma Galgani dedicated her life to the love of Jesus, whose stigmata she bore. She was admitted to the care of the Passionist Fathers, who took not only the three vows of chastity, poverty and obedience, but also a fourth one that committed them to propagateveneration of Christ's Passion. She died in great pain on Easter Saturday, 11 April 1903, and was canonised in 1940.

Stigmata

The *stigmata* are traces in the hands, feet and side of the wounds that Christ suffered during his Passion and Crucifixion. The phenomenon is still the subject of debate, but there are various famous cases of the unexplained appearance of such lesions.

The most famous case is obviously that of St. Francis of Assisi, who in 1224 had a vision of a six-winged seraph hovering in the air before him while he was nailed to a cross just as Christ had been. After that vision came to an end, St. Francis became aware of the marks on his own hands and feet.

Other famous cases include those of St. Catherine of Siena, St. John of God, Padre Pio (1918-1968), Marthe Robin and St. Gemma Galgani. Brother Elie in the Umbrian monastery of Calvi (not far from Rome) is said to bear the marks of the stigmata ever year during the period of Lent.

ROMAN WALL IN THE CHURCH OF SANTA MARIA DELLA ROSA

Sole remnant of Lucca's Roman walls

Via della Rosa - 55100 Lucca (LU)
Visits by appointment only: contact the Congregazione Missionaria Sorelle di Santa Gemma
Casa Giannini. 10, Via del Seminario - 55100 Lucca (LU)
Tel: 0583 48 237
E-Mail: cgianninilucca@libero.it

Lucca is one of the few cities in Italy to maintain intact its original defensive walls, all 4.2 kilometres of them. Built in the 16th and 17th centuries, these Renaissance fortifications now provide the inhabitants with a very pleasant place to stroll and take the air.

Before these ramparts were built, the city had walls dating from the Middle Ages and from Roman times; traces of these still exist, even if they are much less easy to identify.

Among the various remnants of the medieval citywalls (the plural is doubly correct because the fortifications developed over the course of time) are two particularly spectacular city gates: the Porta San Gervasio e Protasio that stands at the corner of Via Santa Croce and Via dei Fossi, and the Porta Borghi, at the end of Via Fillungo.

As for the Roman walls, the local newspapers frequently report that road or building work has unearthed yet more remains of these. However, the only place where an extant section of the walls can be seen by visitors is within the Chapel of Santa Maria della Rosa, in the street of the same name. The Maria della Rosa in question – a Madonna presenting the Christ Child with a rose – appears in a 14th century fresco over the main altar.

The entire left wall of the chapel is part of the old Roman ramparts. Dating from the 2nd century BC, the spectacular wall is made up of opus quadratum – that is, square-cut blocks of stone assembled without mortar. Outside, on the dividing-strip along the street, some blocks of stone have been laid out to indicate the presence of the Roman wall; however, they are not in their original location.

Guided tour of Lucca's three main walls
La Giunchiglia - Lucca Tourist Guides
55100 Lucca (LU)
Tel: 0583 341612 - E-Mail: lagiunchiglia@tin.it
www.lagiunchiglia.net

Cardio-trekking around the city walls

The city council of Lucca has recently come up with an original idea that combines a visit to the town walls and an assessment of your fitness. All you have to do is run (or walk) for 12 minutes, then measure the distance covered thanks to the markers fixed in the ground. Using the table based on the Cooper Test (named after the doctor who devised this "fitness barometer") you can then assess what sort of condition you are in. The table is available free of charge from the Main Tourist Office (Piazzale Verdi - Tel: 0583 583150).

THE MERIDIAN IN THE CHURCH OF SANTA MARIA FORIS PORTAM

A plaque which tells the time...

Piazza Santa Maria Foris Portam
55100 Lucca (LU)

I n Santa Maria Foris Portam (the name recalls the fact that this 12th/13th century church was built outside the gate in the Roman walls) there is a curious plaque on the last column to the right nearest the choir. The inscription reads:

"Passage to Roman Time:

The Equation of Time + 7 minutes and 55 seconds

Difference calculated by Enrico Pucci in 1875

Engraved in marble by the City Council".

On the floor just below it is a meridian in white marble.

In the past, each Italian town determined the time on the basis of local solar time. Then, in the second half of the 19th century, it was decided that there should be a national measure of time based on the meridian of the capital. Known as "Roman time", this was adopted by Milan in 1866, Turin and Bologna in 1867, Venice in 1880 and Lucca in 1875. However, in adapting to the new hour, a precise measurement was required of the difference between previous local time and the new standard – that is, of the difference in longitude between Rome and the city concerned. This is what is commemorated by this plaque in the church of Santa Maria Foris Portam. Enrico Pucci* calculated that since Lucca and Rome varied in longitude by two degrees – 10° 29'E and 12° 29'E respectively – then the Tuscan city had to add 7 minutes 55 seconds to become synchronised with the Italian capital. In doing so, he must have used the meridian that runs across the floor of the nave just in front of the main altar; unfortunately, this no longer functions as a sundial.

Whilst a national Italian time did serve to coordinate activities within Italy, it did not resolve the problems caused by difference in time standards between neighbouring countries. With the advent of railways, postal services and regular shipping, these time differences became increasingly problematical. A full-scale international solution had to be found. By adopting the principle of time zones, the 1884 Washington Conference would set in place a coherent system that still works today.

The Equation of Time

The Equation of Time is the difference between average solar time and real solar time, and can vary during the course of the year. In effect, it is the difference between time as indicated by a sundial and time as given by a clock. This difference is due to the elliptical orbit of the Earth and the inclination of its axis of rotation with respect to the plane of its orbit.

* Enrico Pucci (Lucca 1848 - Florence 1891) was a scientist who specialised in geodesy, the branch of science that determines the exact position of geographical points and studies the shape and size of the Earth.

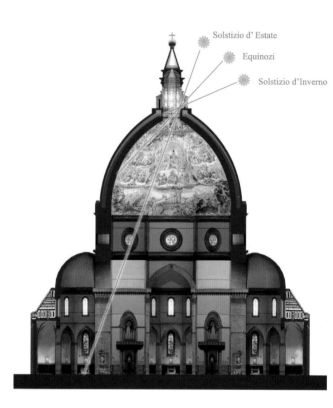

Solstizio d' Estate

Equinozi

Solstizio d'Inverno

How does a meridian work?

Instead of the using the shadow of a gnomon, these use a small hole placed at a certain height, through which the sun's light falls onto a meridian line (i.e. one aligned exactly north-south). The fact that the sun's rays perform the function of the shadow in a traditional sundial means that the opening is sometimes referred to as a "gnomonic opening." The higher the opening, the more efficient the meridian, hence the interest in using cathedrals (see the following section "Why are meridians installed in cathedrals?"); the circumference of the hole had to be no more than one thousandth of the height above the ground. Obviously, the opening had to be installed on the south side of the building in order to let in the rays of the sun, which lies to the south in the northern hemisphere.

The meridian line should run from the point which stands perpendicularly below the axis of the opening, not always easy to determine using the instruments available to scientists in the past (see "The Epic of Ximenes' Meridian"). The length of the line depends on the height of the opening; in some cases, where the building was not long enough to trace the entire meridian line across the floor (as was the case at Saint-Sulpice in Paris), an obelisk was added at its end, so that the movement of the sun's ray could then be measured up the vertical. In summer, when the sun is highest in the sky, the sun's ray falls onto the meridian line closer to the south wall (where that line begins) than it does in winter, when the sun is lower over the horizon and the rays tend to strike towards the far end of the meridian line.

The main principle behind the working of the meridian is that at noon, solar time, the sun is at its apex and, by definition, its rays fall straight along a line running exactly north-south. So, the exact moment when those rays strike the meridian line, which does run north-south, indicates the solar noon. Furthermore, the exact place on the meridian line where that ray falls makes it possible to determine the day of the year: the point right at the beginning of the line is reached solely on the day of the summer solstice, whilst the exact end of the line is reached on the day of the winter solstice. Experience and observation meant that the meridian line could be calibrated to identify different days of the year.

Once this was done, one could use the line to establish the date of various moveable feasts, such as Easter – one of the great scientific and religious uses of meridians. Similarly, one could establish the different periods corresponding with the signs of the Zodiac, which explains where one finds such signs indicated along the length of a number of meridian lines.

Why was 4 october followed immediately by 15 october in the year 1582?

The measurement of time and the origin of the meridians

The entire problem of the measurement of time and the establishment of calendars arises from the fact that the Earth does not take an exact number of days to orbit the sun: one orbit in fact takes neither 365 nor 366 days but rather 365 days, 5 hours, 48 minutes and 45 seconds.

At the time of Julius Caesar, Sosigenes of Alexandria calculated this orbit as 365 days and 6 hours. In order to make up for this difference of an extra 6 hours, he came up with the idea of an extra day every four years: thus the Julian calendar – and the leap year – came into being.

In 325 AD, the Council of Nicaea established the temporal power of the Church (it had been called by Constantine, the first Roman emperor to embrace Christianity). The Church's liturgical year contained fixed feasts such as Christmas, but also moveable feasts such as Easter. This latter was of essential importance as it commemorated the death and resurrection of Christ, and so the Church decided that it should fall on the first Sunday following the full moon after the spring equinox. That year, the equinox fell on 21 March, which was thus established as its permanent date.

However, over the years, observation of the heavens showed that the equinox (which corresponds with a certain known position of the stars) no longer fell on 21 March...The 11 minutes and 15 seconds difference between the real and assumed time of the Earth's orbit around the Sun was resulting in an increasing gap between the actual equinox and 21 March. By the 16th century, that gap had increased to ten full days and so pope Gregory XIII decided to intervene. Quite simply, ten days would be removed from the calendar on 1582, and one would pass directly from 4 October to 15 October... It was also decided, on the basis of complex calculations (carried out most notably by the Calabrian astronomer Luigi Giglio), that the first year of each century (ending in 00) would not actually be a leap year, even though divisible by four. The exceptions would fall every four hundred years, which would mean that in 400 years there would be a total of just 97 (rather than 100) leap years. This came closest to making up the shortfall resulting from difference between the real and assumed time of orbit. Thus 1700, 1800 and 1900 would not be leap years, but 2000 would...

In order to establish the full credibility of this new calendar – and convince the various Protestant nations that continued to use the Julian calendar – Rome initiated the installation of large meridians within its churches. A wonderful scientific epic had begun...

The technical name for a leap year is a bissextile year. The term comes from the fact that the additional day was once placed between 24 and 25 February. In Latin, 24 February was the sixth (sextus) day before the calends of March, hence the name bis sextus, to indicate a supplementary sixth day. The calends were the first day of each month in the Roman calendar.

The meridian of Santa Maria del Fiore: the highest meridian in the world

From the 15th to the 18th century almost 70 meridians were installed in churches in France and Italy. Only ten, however, have a gnomonic opening that is more than 10 metres above floor level – that height being crucial to the accuracy of the instrument:

S. Maria del Fiore (Florence)	90.11 m
S. Petronio (Bologna)	27.07 m
St-Sulpice (Paris)	26.00 m
Monastery of San Nicolo l'Arena (Catania, Sicily)	23.92 m
Cathedral (Milan)	23.82 m
S. Maria degli Angeli (Rome)	20.34 m
Collège de l'Oratoire (Marseille)	17.00 m
S. Giorgio (Modica, Sicily)	14.18 m
Museo Nazionale (Naples)	14.00 m
Cathedral (Palermo)	11.78 m

Why were meridians installed in cathedrals

To make their measurements more precise, astronomers required 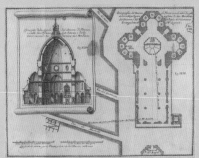 enclosed spaces where the point admitting light was as high as possible from the ground: the longer the beam of light, the more accurately they could establish that it was meeting the floor along an exactly perpendicular plane. Cathedrals were soon recognised as the ideal location for such scientific instruments as meridians. Furthermore, the Church had a vested interest as well, because meridians could be used to establish the exact date of Easter.

The rebellious window jamb of Palazzo Bernardini

Located in the square to which it gives its name, Palazzo Bernardini has one very unusual and inexplicable feature: the right jamb of the ground-floor window to the right of the main doorway has curved and come away from the wall. The protruding base of the jamb is, in fact, held in place by a metal bracket designed to prevent it becoming detached from the wall even further. In itself, this would be nothing remarkable, if it were not for the fact that all of the several attempts to repair or replace the stone have been unsuccessful. It is said that when the palazzo was being built in the 16th century, a religious painting that stood at the site of the jamb was destroyed – and that this mysterious deformation of the window is the result of that act of sacrilege.

Whale plaque on the church of I Servi ⑦

On the façade of the church of I Servi there is a plaque behind a grill which bears an inscription relating to an unusual episode in the city's history. In 1495 a whale was washed up on the shore nearby and its body was then exhibited for the townsfolk in front of this church. The spectacle was forbidden to children, for fear it would cause them to have nightmares...

The eagle of Castruccio Castracani ⑧

At the end of the Cortile degli Svizzeri, within the building that houses the administration of the Province of Lucca, the remnants of the fresco of an eagle can be seen above a portal. This is the emblem of Castruccio Castracani (1281-1328), who after taking and sacking Lucca would subsequently become lord of the city (see below). The present location of the fresco is the result of various alterations to the building, which was originally acquired by Castruccio Casrtracani in 1324. In 1539 the tower which housed a powder magazine blew up after being hit by lightning, causing such extensive damage that the entire palazzo was rebuilt, but various surviving parts of the old structure were retained, including this portal.

The Cortile degli Svizzeri takes it name from the fact that, from 1653 to 1806, it lodged the corps of Swiss soldiers responsible for guarding the palazzo. Recruited in the canton of Lucerne, each of these soldiers had to be a practising Catholic. This decision to hire Swiss soldiers was taken after the treacherous murder of captain Pietro Costantino da Fermo by a member of the previous guard corps, which had comprised fugitive, exiles, and those whose misdeeds were considered to be "crimes of honour."

Castruccio Castracani

Born in Lucca in 1281 to a Ghibelline family, Castruccio Castracani degli Antelminelli was later driven out of the city by the rival faction of the Neri. He then lived as an exile in England, where his valour brought him to the attention of King Edward II, but he had to leave that country after a "crime of honour." Back in Tuscany, he entered the service of Uguccione della Faggiuola, under whom he would take part in the sack of his native city. After various vicissitudes, Castracani was imprisoned by Uguccione, who feared him as a rival. However, when Faggiuola had to flee as a result of popular uprisings in Pisa and Lucca, the people of his native city set Castracani free and appointed him as Captain of the city, then Consul for Life (1316). He spent the remainder of his life administering his territories and resisting the encroachments of Florence and its allies.

SILK MARKS

*Evidence of the time when Lucca was a centre
of silk trade*

Church of San Cristoforo
Via Fillungo - 55100 Lucca
Museo Nazionale di Villa Guinigi. Via della Quarquonia. 55100 Lucca (LU)
Tel: 0583 49 60 33
Opening hours: Tuesday to Saturday 8.30-19.30, Sunday 8.30-13.30
Closed on Monday, Christmas Day, New Year's Day and 1 May
Admission: 4 €, reduced: 2 €, free for those under 18 and over 65
Joint ticket with the Museo Nazionale di Palazzo Mansi: 6.50 €, reduced: 3.25 €

A particularly sharp-eyed visitor might notice a rust mark on the façade of the church of San Cristoforo. Evidence of the time when Lucca was a centre of the silk trade, this was caused by two perpendicular rods of iron which used to serve as standard by which to measure the tools used in making silk. Dating from 1290 and measuring 45 and 86 centimetres respectively, these measures (used in determining the width of combs and looms) are now stored in the Museum of Villa Guinigi. Other silk trade "standards" can be seen at the church of San Frediano (page 175).

From the 11th century onwards, the manufacture and sale of silk was the basis for Lucca's wealth. Given that the pre-eminence of the town depended upon the skill of silk-wavers, their craft was surrounded by mystery and its secrets were under no circumstances to be communicated to outsiders. In order to control and safeguard their craft, weavers and silk-merchants formed a Merchants' Tribunal (Corte dei Mercanti). This met in the church of San Cristoforo at the end of Via Fillungo, which still remains the city's main shopping street.

Silk

Silk is made from the cocoons of the silkworm, which are smothered and then soaked in boiling water in order to kill the chrysalis without damaging the case containing it. The unravelled threads from around a dozen or so cocoons are then spun together to form a single thread of silk. This is strengthened in a subsequent process known as throwing, with the silk being de-gummed (i.e. stripped of remaining mucilage) by being soaked again in boiling soapy water. After that comes the dyeing and weaving. The whole process was developed by the Chinese in the 17th century BC, and the secret would be jealously guarded for almost three thousand years. However travellers (and spies) brought back to Europe information which made it possible to begin copying the technique from around the 6th century AD. With the advent of industrialisation in the 19th century, the manufacture of silk in Europe would almost entirely disappear, in part because of epidemics which killed the silkworms or the mulberry trees on which they fed, in part due to Asian countries taking advantage of these circumstances to reassert a near-monopoly over the silk trade.

MODERN PORTRAITS ON THE FAÇADE OF THE CHURCH OF SAN MICHELE IN FORO

How Cavour and Garibaldi come to find themselves on the façade of a 13th century church...

Piazza San Michele - 55100 Lucca (LU)

The famous church of San Michele in Foro is celebrated by townsfolk and tourists alike; however there are some rather tasty little details about the place which they may not know.

The restoration of the building began in 1866, at the height of enthusiasm for the unification of Italy. Working on the small columns in the upper part of the façade, the craftsmen of the day replaced the badly damaged heads with portraits of contemporary figures – that is, with heroes of the Risorgimento. Thus the sharp-eyed – or those equipped with a good pair of binoculars – can make out Garibaldi (third figure from the right, in the second row from the bottom); Cavour (alongside), King Vittorio Emanuele II (seventh figure from the right), and Mazzini (fourth figure from the left) – not forgetting the great mediaeval poet Dante (sixth from the left).

At little higher up, at the very top of the façade, the large statue of St. Michael holds in its left hand a ring with a red stone which, it is said, reflects the light of the sun into the eyes of anyone who happens to be standing in front of the Banca Commerciale in Piazza San Michele around noon. Legend has it that all those who see this light and make a wish will see it come true…

What is definitely true is that the angel's wings are made up of "mobile" feathers, so that the wind can pass through them and not blow against them as into a sail.

Finally, on the right side of the cathedral, recent restoration work has been careful not to remove the graffiti which over the course of the years was scratched by the market traders who brought their produce here to sell.

Windows for children

Finistrelle are small windows which enabled children to see outside without any risk of falling. A good number of such *finistrelle* can be seen in Piazza del Salvatore (number 9), Corte Portici and Via Calderia (numbers 19 and 21).

MUSEO PAOLO CRESCI AND THE HISTORY OF ITALIAN EMIGRANTS

They Dreamt of "La'Merica"!

Via Vittorio Emanuele, 3 - 55100 Lucca (LU)
Tel: 0583 41 74 83
E-Mail: info@fondazionepaolocresci.it
www.fondazionepaolocresci.it
Opening hours: from 1 October to 30 April, 9.30-12.30 and 14.30-17.30; 1 May
to 30 September, 10.00-12.30 and 15.00-18.30. Closed on Monday
Free admission

Not identified by any sign or plaque on its outside walls, the Museo Paolo Cresci is undoubtedly the least known of the museums in Lucca. It charts the phenomenon of Italian emigration. Comprising the spartan objects used by emigrants – cardboard boxes, robust leather suitcases, bundles, and large bags crammed with souvenirs – the collection gives a very moving picture of how those far from the motherland recreated a sense of home, perhaps within some sort of "Little Italy".* The photographs are a particularly striking record of the brutal reality faced by those who took ship for the long desired 'Merica, where the emigrants first experience would be the harsh immigration controls they had to go through on Ellis Island, beneath the shadow of the Statue of Liberty…

The museum does not provide a nostalgic view of emigration and does not hide the fact that the main motive behind it was poverty. As their only capital was their labour, the immigrants accepted any sort of job, which resulted in them often being looked down upon – be it in the Americas or in France. Trials and tribulations, successes and disappointments, happiness and sadness – the whole mystery of human life is portrayed in this engaging museum.

"An Indulgence of Forty Days for those who say three Hail Marys"

Like a number of other cities in Italy – for example, Palermo – Lucca provides devout Catholics with easily-obtained indulgences for their sins. One sees numerous plaques offering indulgences in the streets and both within and on the exterior of churches. Look, for example, at the side of the church of San Leonardo dei Borghi or at Via del Portico. In the latter case, the indulgence is associated with an ex-voto tabernacle of the Virgin and Child. This was raised in thanks for the safe landing of a child who fell from the fourth floor of a building without serious injury.

The panel reads "Indulgence of Forty Days for those who say three Hail Marys." An indulgence is the total or partial remission granted by God from the pains of Purgatory, and it is obtained by some act of piety (a pilgrimage, prayer, or act of self-mortification) performed in a spirit of repentance. Even if the whole thing may strike many as amazing, belief in this system of indulgences still thrives within the Catholic Church.

* *"Little Italy" was the name given in the United States to the neighbourhoods which contained a concentration of lodgings occupied by Italian immigrants. Overcrowded and uncomfortable, these apartment buildings gave new arrivals the opportunity to provide each other with mutual assistance, and to maintain some of the values and customs of home.*

A YAWNING GULF OF HELL IN THE CHURCH OF SAN AGOSTINO

The Madonna of the Pebble

Piazza San Agostino
55100 Lucca (LU)

The church of San Agostino was built in the 14th century on the site of an old Augustine monastery; its bell-tower incorporates the arches of an ancient Roman theatre. A side chapel in the right aisle has a painting referred to as "The Madonna of the Pebble" because of a miraculous event that astonished the faithful of the time. One day an inhabitant of the city who had just lost a large sum of money gambling was returning home full of bitterness and vented his anger by throwing a pebble at an image of the Virgin. This immediately began to bleed, and a yawning gulf opened up to swallow the unfortunate blasphemer.

The event is commemorated by a plaque in the chapel. Directly below it is an iron trap door over the opening through which the wretched man is said to have fallen straight into Hell…

NEARBY

The Madonna del Soccorso ⑬

Via Fillungo, 215 - 55100 Lucca (LU)

Near Piazza San Pietro, at 215 Via Fillungo, is a raised shrine with an alto rilievo of the Madonna del Soccorso [Our Lady of Succour], in which the Virgin wields a stick to defend the Infant Jesus from the Devil.

The veneration of Our Lady of Succour owes its origins to a miracle that occurred in Sciacca (Sicily), where a mother exasperated at the behaviour of her six-year-old child told him to "go to the Devil." Satan, always on the look-out for such occasions, immediately appeared and seized the child. In response to an appeal for help from the distraught mother, the Virgin appeared robed in white and gold; wielding a club, she then crushed the Devil at her feet whilst protecting the child beneath her cloak. Veneration of Our Lady of Succour was further encouraged by the miraculous healing of the monk Nicolò Bruno (again in Sciacca).

A PHIAL OF CHRIST'S BLOOD IN THE CHURCH OF SAN FREDIANO

A little known but important Christian relic

Piazza San Frediano
55100 Lucca (LU)

If the story of the journey which brought the Holy Visage to Europe is widely told (see page 150), fewer people are aware that the same ship carrying that crucifix from the Holy Land also brought with it phials of Christ's blood.

When the boat ran aground at Luni (Liguria), it was found to contain not only the Holy Visage but also two phials of Christ's blood. One of these was kept for a time at Luni. Later, when the seat of the diocese was moved from that town to Sarzana in 1204, the phial went there too; it is still to be found in the Cathedral dell'Assunta in Sarzana. The second phial is now in Lucca, in the Cenami Chapel in the church of San Frediano (to the right as you enter). A little known but important Christian relic, it is put on display for the faithful only once a year, on Good Friday.

NEARBY

Vestiges of a Roman amphitheatre ⑮
17, Piazza dell'Anfiteatro - 55100 Lucca (LU)

The elliptical shape of Piazza dell'Anfiteatro is due to the fact that the square was laid out on the remaining terraces of a Roman amphitheatre dating from the 2nd/1st century BC. Some of the decoration of that original structure also survives here: at eye-level on the façade of No. 17 one can see a small part of the original decorative frieze. Walking round the square by Via dell'Anfiteatro one can also see some other remnants of the Roman structure: not only some large stone blocks from the base but also some sections of brick partitioning walls.

MONOLITH IN THE CHURCH OF SAN FREDIANO

Faith can move... rocks

Piazza San Frediano
55100 Lucca (LU)

To the left of the high altar in the church of San Frediano is an imposingly large rock of white marble (five metres by two), which has been carved into the form of a rectangular block resting on four feet (two of them the hooves of oxen). A Latin plaque above the stone says "You who read this, whoever you are, you are of stone if this stone does not lead you to admire and venerate San Frediano."

The rock comes from the quarry of San Lorenzo at Vaccoli, on the slopes of the hills between Lucca and Pisa, and its exceptional size made it perfect for the bishop, San Frediano [St. Finnian], who was looking for a single piece of stone to serve as the altar. But a problem arose over how the stone was to be transported, as no one could manage to lift it. It was then that San Frediano miraculously intervened: after intense prayer, he lifted the stone as if it were no more than a sheet of paper and placed it on the cart that was to carry it to its destination. Later, when the church was altered, the block of marble was stored in the sacristy and forgotten. Rediscovered in the 16th century, it was then placed where we see it today.

Note that this was not first miracle performed by the Irish-born St. Frediano: it was he who by means of a simple rake diverted the course of the river Serchio which regularly flooded Lucca.

The first known depiction of the Earth as round

Painted in 1506 by Amico Aspertini, the fresco in the chapel of St. Augustine in the church of San Frediano portrays the journey that brought the Holy Visage from Luni to Lucca (see page 175). When one looks closely, one notes that there are numerous vessels present within the pictorial space and that only the upper parts of the ones furthest away are visible. Furthermore, the line of the horizon is clearly marked so as to accentuate this impression.

It is therefore said that this fresco is the first known representation in art of the rotundity of the Earth. The claim is plausible, given that the fresco was painted in 1506 – that is, 14 years after Christopher Columbus's first voyage to America. The Genoese navigator was, in fact, convinced on that occasion that he had touched land in India, having travelled "to the East via the West". By that time the rotundity of the Earth was a recognised fact amongst the educated and the learned, and was becoming increasingly accepted by the populace at large.

THE WATER TOWERS OF THE LUCCA AQUEDUCT

Aesthetics and engineering

Via del Tempietto - 55100 Lucca (LU)
Via di San Quirico in Guamo Guamo - 55060 Capannori (LU)

The neo-classical water tower/temple at San Concordio, just a short distance from the Lucca city walls, is a structure of rare elegance. Comprising a rotunda and a colonnade, it forms a spectacular composition when viewed along with the arches of the aqueduct that run towards one corner of the structure. Rather more austere (and without a colonnade), the Guamo water tower is built against the hillside. Both bear evidence to the clear importance of aesthetic considerations in the construction of the Lucca aqueduct. Built under the supervision of the architect Lorenzo Nottolini in the period 1823-1851, the aqueduct carries water into the area from the northern slopes of Monte Pisano. After passing through filtering and purifying processes, the water is then stored in the Guamo water tower. The next section of the aqueduct itself is made up of 400 brick arches that stretch for a total of 3,250 metres; however, its continuous line is today interrupted by the motorway. Once the water reaches the San Concordio water tower, it flows into a large marble reservoir from which it then passes to the city via two large steel channels.

The legend of Lucca's Botanical Garden

Legend has it that, on moonless nights, one can hear the lamentations of the ghost of Lucida Manso echoing across the lake within the Botanical Garden. Rich and beautiful, this young woman is said to have chosen her lovers during the course of sumptuous banquets. After having had her way with them, she would then dispose of them by throwing them down a blade-lined well shaft which was hidden beneath a trap-door. Supposedly so narcissistic she even had a mirror concealed in her breviary to admire herself at prayers, Lucida was horrified one day to discover a wrinkle when she inspected her reflection. In despair, she made a pact with the Devil, who appeared to her in the guise of a young man. In exchange for an extra thirty years of youth, she gave him her soul. When the thirty years were about to end, the woman climbed to the top of the clock tower in Via Fillungo in a desperate attempt to stop the clock hands reaching the fatal hour. But the devil caught up with her and took her on a ride around the city walls in a flaming chariot before disappearing with his prize into the lake of the Botanical Garden. Although this may be a legend, Lucida Mansio certainly existed and lived in Lucca during the 17th century. Only 22 years old when her first husband, Vincenzo Diversi, was murdered, she then re-married, but her second spouse, Gaspare Mansi, died shortly afterwards of the plague. It was said that she was beautiful and capricious and had no qualms about taking lovers. No doubt the tale grew out of jealousy, leading certain people to exaggerate accounts of her behaviour.

A STROLL THROUGH ART NOUVEAU LUCCA

The other architectural jewels of Lucca

55100 Lucca (LU)

Famous for its Renaissance city walls, Lucca's numerous Art Nouveau villas have received much less attention.

In 1870 the City council took ownership of the walls and undertook a programme of urban expansion in the areas beyond. The new lots of land were purchased by the local bourgeoisie, who used these sites mainly for building luxurious villas. In a style that varied between the neo-classical and the Art Nouveau, these new districts are well worth a visit, particularly for the villas mentioned below.

The highest concentration of Art Nouveau-style villas is to be found along the southern section of the ring road: Viale G. Guisti, Viale Cavour and Viale G. Carducci. In the latter avenue, note at number 627 a villa decorated with neo-Florentine motifs inspired by the art of the 15th century; today, this is home to the Symphonic Music School. Slightly further on, at nos. 523-545, is a villa whose elegant curve follows a slight bend in the avenue. At the end of Viale Carducci one should not fail to make the detour to Via Pascoli, where at no. 97 there is a superb corner house called Villa Dinelli (formerly Villa Malerbi). Built by Modesto Orzali and his son Gaetano, Villa Ducloz at no. 234 Via Matteo Civitali is a very original structure designed around a large circular panel surrounded by sunflower motifs; the house would subsequently be known as Villa Dianda and is now Villa Barsanti.

Within the city walls a certain number of shops have also preserved Art Nouveau décors. For the central pharmacy, at the corner of Via Beccheria and Piazza San Michele, the ceramicist Umberto Pinzauti created a number of lascivious and at times ambiguous little angels; though in an Art Nouveau style, they are produced using a technique that recalls the work of the Della Robbia family. Passing down the city's main shopping street, Via Fillungo, one often encounters magnificent shop signs and frontages that still reflect the period of the late 19th and early 20th century. See, for example, the Chicchetti jewellery shop at number 219, and the jeweller's and goldsmith's shop, Pellegrini, at No. 111.

One of the least well-known traces of Art Nouveau in Lucca is to be found in the church of San Leonardo in Borghi (Via San Leonardo), where an entire chapel dedicated to the Virgin is decorated in this style.

North West

STANDARD MEASURES FROM THE 16TH CENTURY

Under the loggia, a bushel...

L'Arringo
55051 Barga (LU)

Just to the left of Barga cathedral, the loggia in front of the old Palazzo del Podestà (now the municipal museum) houses standards of weights and measures that were used in the 16th century.

The first of these is the classic Florentine braccia, which measured 58.3 cm. The second is much more unusual and interesting because it reveals a curious fact about this period: people were allowed to walk around carrying daggers and swords, as long as their length respected fixed standards. This measure, known as il coltello (the knife), gives the maximum length of a knife blade at one quarter of a braccia – that is, 14.5 cm.

Two other measures are fixed in the wall and were used to measure dry goods (corn and flour). The largest of these was the *staio fiorentino* (the Florentine bushel) which measured 24.4 litres, whilst the half staio measured 12.2 litres. See Pisa, page 137, for a history of the passage to the metric system and the correspondences between the old weights and measures and the new system.

NEARBY
Symbols in Barga Cathedral ②

Barga's cathedral stands near the Palazzo del Podestà. To the right of its main doorway is a curious stone, no doubt 'recycled' here from its original location. It bears an inscription of certain familiar symbols, but whose significance in this case is rather mysterious. It might, however, be a signature left by the master masons who worked on the cathedral; the same exact inscription is to be found on the Baptistery in Piazza dei Miracoli in Pisa.

THE SUSPENSION BRIDGE TO THE FOUNDRY

One of the longest pedestrian suspension bridges in the world

Between Popiglio and Mammiano Basso (follow the directions to Ponte sospeso delle ferriere)
Open: Always, except at times of high winds
Maximum of 80 people on the bridge at one time

Iron has been produced in Mammiano Basso since 1704, taking full advantage of the River Lima that flows through the hills. But because of the way the valley is configured, the most significant settled areas grew up on the opposite bank at Popiglio. It was as a solution to this problem that Vincenzo Douglas Scotti, an engineer and director of the Mammiano metallurgic establishment, was prompted in 1920 to have a suspension bridge built. The bridge would be built across the valley in order to shorten by several kilometres the workers' daily journey to and from the factory.

In spite of it being a very bold project, it was completed in only two years. All the workers employed in the factory lived locally, and they all worked under the qualified supervision of Scotti in person. Douglas

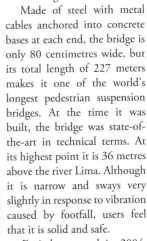

Scotti himself was the designer of the bridge.

Made of steel with metal cables anchored into concrete bases at each end, the bridge is only 80 centimetres wide, but its total length of 227 meters makes it one of the world's longest pedestrian suspension bridges. At the time it was built, the bridge was state-of-the-art in technical terms. At its highest point it is 36 metres above the river Lima. Although it is narrow and sways very slightly in response to vibration caused by footfall, users feel that it is solid and safe.

Entirely restored in 2004, the bridge has not once in all of its years of use witnessed any accidents. It can, of course, cause vertigo, but walking across it will produce a pleasant sense of achievement of the kind experienced after taking a controlled risk — the kind of feeling that engineer Douglas Scotti himself must have experienced more than once in his day.

MUSEUM AND SHELTERS OF THE S.M.I. AT CAMPO TIZZORO

The world's biggest air-raid shelter

Via Luigi Orlando, 325
Campo Tizzoro (Province of Pistoia)
Open: Guided visits start at 10am, 11:30am, 3:30pm and 5pm. Visits last 90 minutes and must be booked in advance. Closed on Tuesdays.
Admission: 10€; 8€ for children aged 6-12 and adults over 65; free for children under 6 years.
Tel: 0573-65724 - Email: rifugismi@irsapt.it

The S.M.I. (Italian Metallurgical Company) was of vital importance during the last two wars because its main production was ammunition. This also made it a favourite target for any enemy. So in 1930 construction began on the world's biggest air-raid shelter: a system of tunnels, stretching out over almost 1,680 metres, excavated straight from the rock more than 20 metres deep, the whole area protected by reinforced concrete a metre thick. The ogive-shaped entrances guaranteed a point of access on the surface, and various technical tricks were employed to ensure that workers and their families could be evacuated from the factory village as quickly as possible.

These tunnels were utilised from 1940 to 1944. They were even equipped with infirmaries, special rooms for the treatment of air and water, a chapel, and in the last year of the war there was even a classroom. There are some intriguing things written on the walls, such as: "Do you know that when walking you use two to five times more air than if you remain quietly seated?"; "In case of unexpected circumstances, self-discipline is the best guarantee of safety"; and even "KEEP CALM. You are already protected in this staircase."

The visit to the tunnels is included in the entry ticket to the museum dedicated to the S.M.I., which did not cease to operate until 2005. The exhibits illustrate how research and innovation were at the heart of the management of the enterprise. You can read the modern rules for safety at work (going back to 1912!) and view the design projects for the construction of the industrial village complex, along with later plans taking us right up to the time of the construction of the shelters.

Also on display is a collection of arms and ammunition, as well as many things in everyday or industrial use that have come about as a result of research into armaments. You will be surprised at how certain alloys now common in the manufacture of musical instruments or even costume jewellery came to be patented.

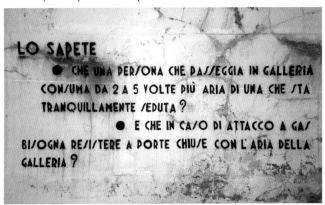

CHESSBOARD OF VICO PANCELLORUM CHURCH

The hermetic game at Saint Paul's church

Village of Vico Pancellorum
Commune of Bagni di Lucca (15 minutes)

Y ou can find traces of the parish church of Vico Pancellorum, a village near Bagni di Lucca, dating from the 9th century although it was substantially rebuilt in the 16th century. In the Middle Ages, documents were also found there attesting to the presence of the Knights Templar.

Above the main entrance is a stunning frieze decorated with sacred figures and a chessboard, the oldest representation in Italy, which has given rise to much speculation and debate without any conclusion being reached as to who was responsible for the carving and what were its purpose and significance.

From left to right, the frieze shows the Christ crucified, a tree, a man with a sword, a chessboard and a Virgin and Child which seems to be a work of the time of the medieval Knights Templar (early 14th century).

The figure of the knight is damaged (it was deliberately obliterated in the past), but you can still see the outline and, although some people take it to be a Knight Templar, it may well be the Apostle Paul, patron saint of this church. That would explain his central position on the portico, especially as the sword he carries matches the traditional descriptions in Christian iconology.

Some people see these figures as allegorical chess pieces: Christ associated with the king, the Virgin with the queen, the Apostle and his sword with the bishop and the knight, the Tree with the rook and the Chessboard with the pawn – all representing the congregation of the faithful who move around the sacred ground of the Church.

Chess is an intellectual game of strategy, both defensive and offensive, military and religious, in the two domains where the Knights Templar were active.

For more information about the origins and the initiatory symbolism of the game of chess, see following double-page spread.

There is also a chessboard on the façade of the church of Sant'Ambrogio in Milan (see *Secret Milan* in this series of guidebooks).

Origins and initiatory symbolism of the game of chess

The word "chess" is derived from the Persian *shah* (king, royal), the Persians claiming to have received the game from India where it was thought to have been introduced in the 6th century AD during the reign of Khosrow I the Just. The game of chess is in fact a sacred invention of the Tibetans to reproduce the cosmic movements of the heavenly and infernal gods on Earth. It came later to India, China and Persia, then Arabia and finally to the Middle East, from where the Crusaders brought it back to Europe in the 13th century.

The number 16 (the number of pieces for each player and the number of horizontal rows and vertical columns) indicates the manifestation of the Spirit over Matter: originally, the game consisted of the triumph over Matter in order to achieve the Enlightenment that will allow the Spirit to conquer a wider consciousness.

The number of squares on the board also has its esoteric meaning: 64 equals four cubed (4x4x4) and eight squared (8x8), which expresses the formal quaternary world consisting of four elements (Air, Fire, Water, Earth) in harmony with one another. Thus the number 64 expresses the present raised to the power of 3, the maximum, i.e. its full expansion.

In the sacred geometry of the ancient Kabbalists, 8, twice 4, is in accord with the quadrature of the circle, in which the octagon is an intermediary between the square and the circle, i.e. between Earth (finite – square) and Heaven (infinite – circle).

As for the chess pieces themselves, the Persians named the queen *pharz* or *ferz* (general). The bishops were known as *fil* (elephant), a name that has survived in Spanish as *alfiln*, derived from the Latin *arphillus*, and appears again in Old French as *auphin* or *dauphin*. In the *Roman de la rose* (13th century), these two pieces are mentioned for the first time by their modern French names. Because the bishops are placed next to the king and queen, the Arabs of Spain at the time of Alfonso the Wise gave them the name *alferez* (aides-de-camp), from which the Italians derived *alfiere* (*alferes* in Portuguese). Finally, in England they evolved into bishops and in Germany, *Läuferns* (runners). The knights are the same in all these languages except German, where they are known as *Springers* (jumpers).

In Persia, the rook was represented by an elephant carrying armed men on its back, but the Arabs replaced it with a bird (the *roc*), from which is derived the French verb *roquer* (to castle), a defensive chess move in which the king and the rook are allowed to move at the same time. Finally, in Persia the pawn was known as a valet or infantryman. The Italian *pedone* is a derivative, as are the Spanish *peón* and the Portuguese *peão*. The Germans call this piece *Bauer* (peasant) and the English infantryman or pawn.

In chess, each piece moves in a different way. The king moves in any direction, but only one square at a time: even while "Lord of the Universe", one can only conquer Matter square by square, little by little. The queen moves in all directions, and as the Lady of Matter she can move (if nothing prevents her) from one end of the board to the other. The bishops can only move diagonally, which represents the line between Earth and Heaven: they are the intermediaries between the two worlds. The rooks move in both vertical and horizontal directions, the expression of heavenly Enlightenment and terrestrial Initiation. The knights move, so to speak, in a square, expressing dynamic Initiation within the quadrature of matter. The pawns can only jump over the squares next to theirs, indicating that they have taken a step in the Game of Initiation. The king, the main piece, cannot be taken: when he is in check, he is obliged to make a move. He heralds the crisis of Initiation which at the beginning invades the neophyte. But when the king can no longer move without incurring a new danger, indicating a moral and intellectual failure in the neophyte's Initiation, he is said to be checkmate (from the Arabic math, death) and the game is over.

THE ABANDONED THERMAL BATHS OF KINGS

The good old days when pampering was a guarantee of health

Bagni di Lucca (Province of Lucca), various locations
Admission: Visits are free when available
Tel: 3282-732-703 - Email: vicaria.valdilima@hotmail.com

The story of Bagni di Lucca rightly deserves to be told. The little town sits in a valley on the river Lima, which is not blessed with a great deal of sunshine. As soon as you enter it you sense an atmosphere of past decadence. You will be struck by the presence of fine mansions, villas and hotels. Sadly these are, for the most part, abandoned. Your curiosity aroused, you will soon find out that this spa resort was once one of the most important in Europe for a period spanning several centuries. It is because of Bagni di Lucca that the Republic of Lucca managed to avoid getting embroiled in a number of wars over the years – sovereigns who were regular visitors insisted that they should not be deterred from coming here to relax, take their cures and generally have fun. Apart from the fact that the waters boast excellent therapeutic qualities, the other important explanation for Bagni di Lucca's success is its toleration of gambling (see below). As far back as 1308, references are made to games of chance in early regulations relating to the running of a spa – *ludus in therma*. This is where the predecessor of roulette has its origins. It was called *biribosso* and even women were allowed to indulge in the game. The first casino was opened in Bagni di Lucca too. Sadly, the closure of the gaming houses brought about the town's decline as they gradually pulled out. In the glorious centuries when activity was at its most intense, there were around eight hotels, three casinos and seven bathing establishments. Only two of the latter are now operating, the others having been abandoned. However, two have been recently restored and can be visited upon request. The highlights of these are their marble pools, grottos and steam rooms, as well as the old inscriptions on view there. As an added bonus, historical association volunteers will enthusiastically reveal to you the spa's many secrets.

The waters of Bagni di Lucca – rainwater that comes back up to the surface forty years later

The process starts when rainwater, with its gamut of therapeutic qualities, permeates the surface of one of the hills of the region and reappears 40 years later as it flows from a number of springs, each with different characteristics. On its way, the water filters down, later to rise up through a radioactive basin of 3 to 4 million cubic metres at a temperature of 70 °C. The water follows various natural conduits that bestow on it a wide variety of mineral properties. Alas, some of the springs cannot be harnessed, and even today much of the hot and/or curative spring water simply disappears into the river.

THE BRANCOLINO ON
THE CHURCH OF SAN GIORGIO

*Who is that odd character on the Church
of San Giorgio?*

Pieve di Brancoli, 55100 Lucca (LU)

According to some sources, the church of San Giorgio in Pieve di Brancoli was first founded in 722; what is certain is that there was a church here in 1097.

Above the side door to the right of the church there is a carved figure that does not fit in with the usual iconography of religious sculpture. Nicknamed Il Brancolino (from the verb meaning "to grope one's way"), this unusual bas-relief is still a mystery. The most likely explanation offered nowadays is that it was carved as a joke by one of the stone-masons who built the church.

The legend of the Devil's Bridge

Ponte del Diavolo or Ponte della Maddalena. 55023 Borgo a Mozzano (LU)

The spectacular humpback bridge over the river Serchio has five arches in all; the one at the end was added more recently to span the local rail line. The nickname Ponte del Diavolo comes from a legend dating from the time of its construction in the 14th century. Work had fallen behind schedule and so the architect – fearing he would not meet the deadline – called for help from the Devil. Lucifer agreed to complete the structure overnight as long as it was agreed he could carry off the soul of the first person to cross the bridge. Stricken with remorse, the architect confessed what he had done to the village priest, who hit upon a solution: a pig would be the first living creature to cross the bridge... Furious, the Devil disappeared into the river beneath in a cloud of sulphur. It is also said that the Devil later got his revenge by making sure that there were constant increases in the toll required to cross the bridge.

CRYSTALS ASSOCIATED WITH CARRARA MARBLE

Diamond in marble

The Fornaci di Barga Mineralogy and Palaeontology Group
Via Galilei Galileo
55051 Fornaci di Barga (LU)
Tel: 0583 758 879
Visits by appointment only
Free admission

While the main attraction of other marbles is their variety of colour, Carrara marble has the unique characteristic of being of a very pure white. This means that the stone brings out all the magnificence of any other minerals found within it – particularly if these are crystallised. These juxtapositions form striking visual contrasts and are much sought after by collectors and enthusiasts of natural curios.

Founded in 1973, the Fornaci di Barga Mineralogy and Palaeontology Group specialises in the search for such mineral combinations within local marble. On its premises there is an exceptional collection of some 50 different types, along with fossils and minerals from all over the world.

One exhibit is a superb piece of rock crystal occurring within a milky white chunk of marble; the stunning contrast of the two materials reminds one of the mysterious chances at work in natural creation. Another exhibit is a crystal of pure sulphur (unmixed with other elements); bright yellow in colour, this stands out against the marble like a flower under ice.

The honorary president of the Group, Raffaleo Lucchesi, is happy to open the museum to visitors (by prior appointment). Far from being too busy to assist, he welcomes the chance to give you a knowledgeable tour, and – photos in hand – will gladly tell you where he and his friends found these natural wonders.

PINOCCHIO'S OAK TREE

Pinocchio could well have been hanged from the branches of this hundred-year oak

Il Quercione (literally, The Great Oak)
Via Carrara. Wood of San Martino in Colle – 55012 Capannori (LU)

Known as "Pinocchio's oak" or *Il Quercione*, this remarkable tree is over 600 years old and is thought to have inspired Collodi, author of the famous children's story, for the scene of Pinocchio's hanging by the Cat and the Fox. Unfortunately the tree is now endangered by parasites, and the municipality of Capannori has recently launched a campaign to save it – supported, among others, by Roberto Benigni, director of one of the latest film adaptations of Pinocchio.

For more on Pinocchio, see following double-page spread.

NEARBY
The plaque and the magnolia of the Swiss guards ⑩
Piazza Vittorio Emanuele - 55011 Altopascio (LU)

In September 1505, 150 Swiss halberdiers left Bellinzone in the Swiss canton of Tessin for Rome, called there by Pope Julius II. They would arrive in the city on 22 January 1506, becoming the first body of the Papal Swiss Guard.

In 2006, to commemorate the five-hundredth anniversary of the creation of that Papal Guard, the 720-kilometres march was repeated by 70 former Swiss Guards. At each stopping-point on their route, a plaque was placed by a tree. Under the magnolia in Piazza Vittorio Emanuele, the plaque records that on 20 April 2006 the march reached its 14th stopping-place at Altopascio, having already covered some 293 kms.

Pinocchio: the first Masonic puppet

Though not officially recognised, Carlo Collodi's membership in the Freemasons is widely believed to be confirmed by a range of evidence: he started a satirical newspaper entitled *Il Lampione* (The Lamp Post) in 1848, with the express aim of "illuminating all those held in thrall by the shadows"; his participation in the campaigns of Giuseppe Garibaldi, a famous *carbonaro* advocating liberal ideas and undoubtedly a Mason; his close relationship with Mazzini, who was a well-known Mason and of whom Collodi declared himself to be a "passionate disciple". Furthermore, the guiding principles of the Freemasons – *Liberty*, *Equality* and *Fraternity* – are embodied in *The Adventures of Pinocchio*: Liberty, because Pinocchio is a free being, who loves liberty; Equality, because Pinocchio's sole aspiration is to be equal to everyone else, accepting that all are born equal to each other; Fraternity, because this is the feeling that seems to motivate the characters at various points in the story. *Pinocchio* was also immortalised in a film by the American Walt Disney, himself a high-ranking Mason, and embodies the three founding principles of universal freemasonry: freedom of thought and will; psychological and social equality; fraternity between individuals, who can thus achieve universal understanding. More than a simple children's story, *Pinocchio* is an initiatory tale, as is Goethe's *Faust* and Mozart's *The Magic Flute*. It can be read at various levels as a Masonic parable, with the multiple meanings reflecting themes and formulas associated with the stages of initiation. Indeed, it is due to these veiled allusions to an initiatory path that Pinocchio owes its extraordinary success (its sales in twentieth-century Italy were second only to those of *La divina commedia*), for the various stages in the plot offer subliminal echoes of cognitive archetypes. A formidable didactic instrument, *Pinocchio* takes its place alongside the official educational literature of its day. A moral tale deeply imbued with the message of political emancipation, it is one of Tuscan culture's greatest contributions to Freemasonry. Pinocchio is subject to a long course of development. Initially nothing more than a "rough" piece of wood (just like the "rough" stone that all the uninitiated have to cut and shape), he must become "polished" (a term which in the Masonic vocabulary means "enlightened"). The very name of Pinocchio derives from *pinolo*, the Italian word for "pine nut", thus there is a connection with pine trees, traditionally associated with Christmas – and Christmas itself is a symbol of the spiritual rebirth that the neophyte will experience when he receives the light of initiation. Furthermore, it is no coincidence that the central character of the tale, Geppetto, is a carpenter, as was Joseph, the father who raised Jesus Christ. As a carpenter, Geppetto is also a demiurge ("creator", "artisan") in the Platonic and Gnostic sense of the term. A little later in the tale, the Blue Fairy descends from heaven to teach Pinocchio free will, and when he asks if he has finally become a real boy she significantly answers: "No, Pinocchio. The vow of your father Geppetto will not fully come true until you deserve it. Set yourself to the test, with courage, sincerity and passion, and one day you will become a real little boy." This is precisely what is said during Masonic initiation, with regard to apprenticeship and the bearing of responsibility. The voice of the Cricket is definitely that of conscience, urging the puppet to go "to school" – another Masonic symbol for conscience and awareness. The initiation of Pinocchio also comprises a series of trials that involve all four elements: air (the presence of numerous birds in the story, and the puppet's flight on the wings of a dove); earth (the coins buried in the ditch); fire (which burns his feet) and water (with various episodes, right up to the final chapter, involving swimming and drowning). Pinocchio is also prey to "sleep", another Masonic metaphor for the non-activity of the uninitiated; and it is precisely when he is asleep that the Blue Fairy gives him a kiss (a kiss also being part of the Masonic rite of the Templars). When hanged, Pinocchio dies, but he is resuscitated through a purge/purification – that is, by elevating himself to a higher level of initiation. Among the other references to Freemasonry there is the island of industrious bees, which recalls Hiram's Temple of Solomon, with its four hundred pomegranates. That is also the exact number of the small bread buns which the Blue Fairy prepares together with cups of coffee and milk (the colour contrast of black and white is another feature of the Temple and a symbol of the contrast between good and evil). The Cat, the Fox and the Firefly all embody the temptations of an easy and profane life, with limping and lameness being other allusions to Masonic symbols. The puppeteer Stromboli and the Land of Toys again represent the vanities of this world, and Pinocchio's transformation into a donkey reveals he has fallen to the level of beasts. To save himself, he must return to the path of enlightenment. The puppet must find his father/demiurge, but he can only do so after passing through a biblical trial: being swallowed by a whale like Jonah, the central figure in a myth that is fundamental in all the great monotheistic religions and all schools of esotericism. Being reunited with Geppetto, who bears him on his shoulders as he swims through the primary element of water, Pinocchio finally becomes a "real little boy", one of the truly "enlightened".

A PERFECT COPY OF THE
MADONNA DEL BALDACCHINO

A certain air of déjà vu

Cathedral of Pescia
Piazza Duomo

Turning into the last chapel on the right (the Turini Chapel), visitors might begin to wonder: "I'm sure I've seen that painting someplace else!" And you may have very well seen it before: in the Pitti Palace in Florence. The story behind this magnificent copy of Raphael's Madonna del Baldacchino is rather amusing. At the beginning of the 16th century, Cardinal Baldassare Turini, a native of Pescia, commissioned Raphael to paint a picture for the church of Santa Maria Assunta in his native town. In 1507 the painting was given a triumphant reception by the faithful and thereafter became the pride of the church.

However, in 1697, Prince Fernando de Medici, the eldest son of Grand Duke Cosimo III and a great lover of art, visited Pescia and was left thunderstruck by Raphael's masterpiece. To persuade the local clergy to let him have it, he offered not only the immense sum of 1,000 scudi but also commissioned the talented artist Pietro Dandini to paint a copy that was as close as possible to the original. The two paintings were then switched - in great secrecy - during the night of 7 September 1697.

The local clergy later used the money they had received to install a church organ and to extend their library.

NEARBY
Meridian in the cathedral of Pescia ⑫
Piazza del Duomo

The improvements carried out thanks to the money received from Prince Ferdinand (see above) also affected the large sundial meridian that runs across the floor of the church. Whilst part of the white marble line is still visible, one now has to open the door in the enclosure beneath the organ to see it in its entirety. The hole by which sunlight entered the church and fell onto the meridian had already been moved during the course of previous building work, so that the sundial was even then no longer as precise as it had once been.

A DA VINCI ANGEL

One of Leonardo da Vinci's two known works of sculpture

Church of San Gennaro
Via Ilio Menicucci
55010 San Gennaro (LU)
To visit, ask at the presbytery, to the left of the church

Standing on the steep main road that runs through the hills above Lucca, the village of San Gennaro is not far from Collodi (which provided the writer Carlo Lorenzini, author of The Adventures of Pinocchio, with his penname). Re-built in the 12th century, the church of San Gennaro would in 1998 become an unusual focus of attention for the world's media. In an article published in the Italian newspaper Il Sole 24 ore, Professor Carlo Pedretti of UCLA, the greatest living expert on Leonardo da Vinci, would attribute the statue of a angel in San Gennaro to that artist.

The revelation was something of a scoop, as at the time there was only one known work of sculpture by Leonardo da Vinci: that of the Christ Child, now kept in the vaults of a bank in Rome.

This polychrome terracotta statue of an angel had in 1958 been attributed to the "School of Verrocchio" by Prof. Lodovico Ragghianti, an art historian and critic. Given that the young Leonardo learnt his craft in Verrocchio's studio, Ragghianti was not that far off the presently

accepted attribution. The basis for identifying this statue as an early work by Leonardo is its striking similarity with his sketch "Study for the Sleeve of the Angel of the Annunciation" which is now in the Uffizi in Florence.

What remains a mystery is how this work by Leonardo da Vinci ended up in this modest village. However that came about, there are records of its presence here from 1772 onwards: archives record that the statue was damaged that year by a falling ladder. Having been restored on that occasion by a local artist, the statue still retains all its charm.

THE EMBLEM OF THE ORDER OF THE CROSS OF SAINT ANTHONY

The order of the Tau

Piazza Ospitalieri
55011 Altopascio (LU)

A sign on the A11 motorway (Firenze-Mare) which informs drivers that they are approaching the town of Altopascio mentions "bread and board" (pane e ospitalità). This was, in fact, a traditional service offered by Altopascio, a necessary stopping-point on the ancient Via Francigena (see page 74). One can still see various important reminders of this past function in the town's historic centre

In various places there are traces of the emblem associated with the Knights of the Order of St. Anthony: the Greek "T" or Tau (see box feature below). The first of these (a large stone from the knights' old hospital) is on the balcony of the Municipal Library overlooking Piazza Ospitalieri; the building is entered by a staircase that runs down into the large Piazza Vittorio Enmanuele. There are also several other Greek Ts, together with ancient carved inscriptions, to be found on the stone facing of the north side of the church bell tower.

Knights of the Order of the Cross of Saint Anthony

The Altopascio Hospital was founded in the 11th century; some argue the tenth. It was intended to offer board, food and care for the numerous pilgrims taking this road on their way to the tomb of St. Peter in Rome (then perhaps continuing to the Holy Land) or, travelling in the other direction, on their way to Santiago di Compostella. So that these travellers would not lose their way in the unhealthy marshlands of this area, at nightfall the local bell tower (still in use today) rang La Smarrita, which take its name from the verb "to go astray." Due to the fact that travellers were preyed upon by brigands and bandits, the Augustinian monks who ran the hospital soon had to arm themselves in order to provide protection. This was the origin of the oldest military order in the world: the Hospitaller Knights of the Cross of Saint Anthony, also known as the Order of the Tau because of the Greek "T" that was their symbol. The symbol was traced in white on the left side of the black or grey robes worn by the Knights. The Tau was a symbol of both the pilgrim's staff and the Cross of Christ.

Altopascio still maintains its reputation for hospitality; the town has eight free places to provide board for pilgrims and visitors to its monasteries. Contact the Tourist Office (10, Piazza Garibaldi - 55011 Altopascio (LU); tel: 0583 21 65 25; e-mail: turismo@ comune.altopascio.lu.it) or the local library (23, Piazza Vittorio Emanuele; tel: 0583 21 62 80; e-mail : biblioteca@ comune. altopascio.lu.it).

CROSS OF THE PASSION IN THE CHURCH OF SAN PIETRO IN GRADO ⑮

A Cross with the instruments of Christ's Passion

Basilica of San Pietro al Molo
5, Via Vecchia di Marina - 56010 San Piero a Grado (PI)
Tel: 050 960065
Opening hours: 8.00-19.00
Free admission

Supposedly built on the exact site where St. Peter the Apostle came ashore after his voyage from Palestine, the church of San Pietro in Grado is curious for a number of reasons. Firstly because it has no actual façade; for unknown reasons, at the end of the 12th/beginning of the 13th century its nave was shortened by a quarter, with the demolished facade being replaced by an enclosed apse. Another curiosity is that the site of the church, now located five kilometres inland, was once a quayside in Pisa, a busy maritime port since Roman times - that is, until gradual silting along the Arno shifted the mouth of the river further west, thus putting an end to the port's usefulness. Inside the church, opposite and a little to the right of the main door, is a very interesting Cross said to date from the 18th century. It is complete with a rare – and surprisingly realistic – depiction of the instruments of the Passion: the hammer, the sponge soaked in vinegar, the Vernicle (a handkerchief impressed with the image of Christ's face), the spear, the ladder, the crown of thorns, the pitcher and bowl used by Pilate when washing his hands, the whip, the red tunic, the chalice, the dice cast by the Roman soldiers and the panel bearing the inscription "INRI" [Jesus of Nazareth, King of the Jews]. The only things missing are the nails. Another Cross with a powerful evocation of the Passion is to be seen at Montecatini Alto (see page 25).

The port of Pisa wiped off the map

Porto Pisano, the ancient port of Pisa, dated back at least as far as the 6th century BC; archaeological evidence shows that by this period the city was trading with the Greeks, the Phoenicians, and the Gauls.

The docks of the port ran from just north of modern-day Livorno to the vast estuary of the Arno and the Auser (a river that has since run dry) in an area that has now silted up. Jealously protected by the maritime republic, the port played a major role in the development of Pisa; it was defended by four immense towers that were destroyed by the Genoese during the battle of La Meloria in 1290 but then rebuilt in 1297-1310. However, pressure from foreign naval powers and conflicts with neighbouring cities and rivals initiated a long period of decline for Pisa. The port did continue to function, but less and less attention was devoed to the upkeep of the docks. Finally, the Florentine conquest of Pisa in 1509 and the decision to build the new port of Leghorn [Livorno] delivered the coup de grâce. Without regular maintenance, the port gradually silted up thanks to the alluvial deposits left by the Arno. Now, less than five centuries later, the sea is some 5 km from the original coastline.

THE ORNITHOLOGICAL MUSEUM AT TORRE DEL LAGO ⑯

A truly idyllic spot

Inside the Gran Teatro all'Aperto Giacomo Puccini
Via delle Torbiere, Torre del Lago Puccini (Province of Lucca)
Visits to the museum and requests to visit can be made during the opening hours
of the theatre or its offices - Tel: 0584-350-567 - www.puccinifestival.it

It is well known that Giacomo Puccini drew inspiration from the lake of Massaciuccoli — he even owned a villa there. The works of the great composer are performed in the magnificent open-air theatre built on the shore of the lake in this wonderful place every summer on the occasion of the Festival Puccini. This annual event dedicated to the composer has been staged for a number of decades. What is less well known about the lake is that it is a habitat to a great many natural species. A local hunter named Galò was so inspired by this that he bequeathed his personal collection of stuffed birds to the village. It includes a wide range of species, both native to the lake and migratory — about one hundred different birds in all. The collection also includes a replica of the traditional small fishing boat used on the lake. It was made strictly in accordance with ancient boat-building techniques by members of the U.O.E.I. hiking club, which promotes the nature and history of the area on a voluntary basis. The wooden craft traditionally has a flat bottom and is equipped with a supply of paddles to enable fishermen and game hunters to manoeuvre it on the lake, as well as the canals and marshes that have stamped their character on the area. The lake is still noted for its wide variety of fauna and flora.

NEARBY
The Villa Orlando

Viale Puccini 252 - Tel: 0584 341 886 - www.villaorlando.it

This fine private residence is open to visitors during two periods each year, in

May and September. It is particularly notable for its park, with its rich variety of traditional plants, the tree-lined path leading up to the villa, and the northern European style of the villa's architecture. It was built in 1869 by businessmen from Alsace who brought with them to the lakeside a style of architecture much more commonly seen in France. The entry to the villa is recognisable by the ruins of faux medieval towers. The Germans demolished these during the war, since after turning the villa into their headquarters, they realised the towers were too much visible. On the outside walls, the remains of pictures of warships, unfortunately damaged, can still be seen. These were used to by soldiers to assist in distinguishing between craft of the Allies and those of the enemy.

Torre del Lago's very own "La Bohème"

The original village, that is to say the part of Torre del Lago that overlooks the lake, only consists of a handful of buildings, although some of these, like the Villa Orlando, are high value properties. It is probably because of its size and location that it became for a time a hub for culture and creativity. As well as Puccini, a number of painters, such as Ferruccio Pagni and Francesco Fanelli, were drawn to this place. The artists here lived life to the full as regular patrons of the dive restaurant once located on the lake's edge. They rechristened this meeting place the La Bohème Club. To give some idea of the nature of the Club, we reproduce its "rules" below:

Art. 1 Members of the La Bohème Club, in accordance with the spirit in which the Club was founded, undertake to maximise their intake of food and drink.

Art. 2 Grumpies, prigs, problematic eaters, half-wits, fusspots and other sad people of that kind are not admitted as they risk being furiously ejected by the members.

Art. 3 The president holds the office of mediator, but he has a duty to obstruct the treasurer in matters regarding the collection of Club dues.

Art. 4 The treasurer retains the right to flee with the takings.

Art. 5 Lighting of the establishment is provided by way of oil-lamps. If fuel runs low, the Club shall have recourse to requisitioning candles belonging to members of the Club.

Art. 6 Legal games are strictly forbidden. Art. 7 Silence is not permitted.

Art. 8 Good sense is not permitted even on an exceptional basis.

You can still see some of these artists' frescoes in the Chalet del Lago restaurant — Tel: 0584-359-830, www.chaletdellago.it

MONUMENT TO THE VIAREGGIO DEEP-SEA DIVERS (18)

Pioneers in the recovery of sunken cargo

Lungo Canale Palombari dell'Artiglio
55049 Viareggio (LU)

With advances in the technique and technology of deep-sea diving, people began to contemplate the possibility of recovering cargoes lost in shipwreck at sea. In 1925 a company was founded in Genoa to carry out such deep-water salvage, and nearly all the divers it employed would come from Viareggio.

The first attempted salvage – involving the diving ship Artiglio – was only half-successful, but it attracted a lot of attention because the divers shattered the existing record for deep-water submersion, reaching a depth of 136 m. Their intention had been to recover the twelve tons of ivory tusks and 13,000 carats of diamonds which had been on board the Elisabethville, a ship torpedoed by a German U-Boat in 1917. Only the ivory was brought up to the surface; of the diamonds, no trace.

In 1930 the company suffered the tragic loss of the Artiglio, along with its crew and all divers, during a mission to destroy the cargo of munitions that had been on board the American ship Florence.

The Viareggio divers' greatest triumph, however, would come shortly afterwards, when they recovered part of the gold that had been in the hold of the English ship Egypt, that sank off the coast of Brittany. A packet boat that travelled from London to Bombay, the ship had collided in thick fog with the French cargo vessel La Seine in 1922. Thanks to the diving-bell designed by head diver Alberto Gianni and engineer Roberto Galeazzi, the divers on Artiglio II managed to bring to the surface a total of 856 ingots. Amongst the other operations in which they were involved, one that deserves anecdotal mention is the refloating of Giacomo Puccini's yacht, the Ciò Ciò San.

The Diving-Bell

The monument in Viareggio includes one of the diving-bells used in the deep-sea recoveries. The bell was lowered by cable directly above the wreck. Inside, the diver communicated with the surface via phone, guiding a scoop operated by a crane. In the case of the Egypt, the ship's strongroom had to be blown open using explosives, again following instructions provided by the diver in the bell.

ARCICONFRATERNITÀ DELLA MISERICORDIA

⑲

The façade of the Misericordia di Viareggio

97, Via Cavalotti - 55049 Viareggio (LU)
Don't forget to take one of the free leaflets on "Art Nouveau in Tuscany: Itineraries
of Architecture dating from 1880 to 1930", available in the Viareggio Tourist Office
Tourist Office. APT Versilia
10, Viale Carducci - 55049 Viareggio (LU)
Tel: 0584 96 22 33
E-Mail: aptversilia@versilia.turismo.toscana.it
www.versilia.turismo.toscana.it

The volunteers of the *Arciconfraternità de la Misericordia di Viareggio* seem rather surprised to see people taking photographs of their premises, which stand some way back from the seafront in a quiet little street; clearly they are used to the beauty of this building's façade. Created by the ceramicists of Galileo Chini's "Fornaci de San Lorenzo," the frontage is quite simply remarkable. On the left, a woman turns towards the past and towards the Cross (which serves as a sort of framework for the entire design), while to the right a woman looks towards the present and seems to be protecting a child. The entire work is in the flamboyant style of Galileo Chini at his most creative.

Viareggio is undoubtedly the Tuscan town with the richest concentration of Art Nouveau architecture; forty or so buildings are listed in the leaflet provided by the Tourist Office. But the terrible fire of 1917 destroyed almost all the wooden buildings along the seashore, with the sole exception of the Padiglione Martini. Having acquired jurisdiction over the seafront, in 1924 the town council decided to redevelop it in a very opulent fashion. A member of the committee of architects responsible for coordinating the scheme, Chini (see below) would leave his own very distinctive mark on the entire project.

Galileo Chini

Born in Florence in 1873, Galileo Chini – painter, graphic artist, architect, interior decorator, ceramicist, and set-designer – is considered the most important exponent of Art Nouveau in Italy. After having set up his Arte della Ceramica company for the production of art ceramics in 1896, he would branch out in 1904 by founding I Fornaci di San Lorenzo [Ceramic Kilns of San Lorenzo]. Comprising ceramics, mosaics, glass and also furnishings that incorporated them, Galileo Chini's work would enjoy extraordinary success and win various design awards. In the 1930s Chini would dedicate himself to painting, after having decorated the Throne Room in the Palace of Bangkok; he would also design sets for Puccini's Turandot. He died in Florence in 1956.

The Art Nouveau-style holiday home that he had built for himself at Lido di Camaiore has been preserved and is now a charming little hotel and restaurant: Hotel Villa i Pini, 43, Via Roma - 55043 Lido di Camaiore (LU). Tel: 0584 66 103. E-mail: info@clubipini. com. Site internet : www.clubipini.com. Rooms from 50 A to 170 A. Dinner: 25 A per person (served in the garden upon request).

AN ASCENT ALONG
THE PIASTRETA MONORAIL

The incredible marble cable car

Renara, outside Gronda - 54100 Massa-Carrara (MS)
The "engine" is on display outside the office of the Ezio Ronchieri Marble Works.
It is advisable to phone or send an e-mail beforehand. However, the workcrew
are very happy to show off the wonderful engine for visitors!
16, Via Boschetto. 54100 Massa-Carrara (MS)
Tel: 0585 41 262
E-mail: info@ezioronchieri.com

In quarrying the famous marble of Massa Carrara, the problem faced by the Ronchieri company was how to get large blocks of immaculate white marble down from an altitude of 1,800 metres. They came up with a spectacular solution: for fifty years – from 1922 to 1972 – the engine now displayed at the entrance to the Ronchieri Marble Works transported blocks of marble weighing up to 12 tons along a monorail that at some points attains a gradient of 80%. The engine was driven by a 22-horsepower motor with five speeds, a reverse gear and pneumatic caterpillar tracks.

The route of the monorail can now be followed on foot. It provides wonderful views, but is not recommended for young children.

Directions: From Massa-Carrara drive towards Gronda. Just before the village, turn right to Renara. Drive for 500 metres until the road comes to an end. Here you are at the point where two mountain streams meet; they are dry in summer. Cross the stream that flows down on your right and then go up the slope on your left, turning to the right of the ruined houses. This brings you to the lower end of the monorail, even if at this level the rail itself has now disappeared. The track looks like a railway line whose two rails have been cemented. Things begin to get more serious once you reach an altitude of 500 metres, with the monorail ascending to 1,800 metres after a steep climb of over three kilometres. Progress over this last part is by means of the steps (2,000 of them!) that run alongside the rail.

A ramble along Via Vandelli

Via Vandelli, a historic road linking Modena with the sea, was laid out at the behest of Francesco III d'Este, Duke of Modena (1698- 1780), with the purpose of linking his capital with Massa-Carrara and the sea. The main problem was that the road had to keep within his Duchy and not stray into the neighbouring territories of the Papal States, the Duchy of Lucca or the Grand Duchy of Tuscany. The monk Domenici Vandelli, a geographer and mathematician, was commissioned to chart the road, which was to cross the Apennines at the Tambura Pass (some 1,634 m above sea level). After 13 years of intense work (1738-1751), the road was completed; but it was never used much because of exposed weather conditions and the fact that the surrounding countryside was infested with bandits and brigands. Today, the road is being restored and the route from Resceto to the Tambura Pass is popular with ramblers. A monument placed at the beginning of Via Vandelli commemorates the epic of its creation.

THE TERZO QUARRIES

A marble quarry not normally accessible to the public

B&B La Cava di Terzo
Casette area (Province of Massa-Carrara)
Open: When the quarry is in operation, visits are free for guests at the B&B,
except on Sundays or when weather conditions prevent them.
Tel: 335-776-1775
Email: mario.ricci1@gmail.com

The family name Ricci de Casette is widespread in the region and is the name of the oldest family of quarry workers still active in Carrara. The current generation is the sixth in the family's quarrying history, which started back in 1900 when their great-great-grandparents (including one Terzo Ricci) were involved in large-scale working of the mountain using dynamite. Things have changed a lot since then, of course, but the family is still actively involved almost entirely in the extraction of marble. And guests at their bed and breakfast can ask to accompany them to one of their working quarries — an adventure not usually available to the public.

One such quarry is situated close to the family's home where some rooms have been converted to receive visitors. A few phone calls to a relative ... and the number of people interested in visiting the quarry and details of what transport is needed to get there is agreed. An off-road vehicle is essential for the last part of the journey. These visits are unforgettable, not only because of where they take place, but also because they are brought to life by the guide's first-hand stories and on-site explanations of how the marble is extracted from the mountain.

How is the mountain quarried?

Marble was already being extracted from the Apuan Alps in Roman times. Indeed, the mountain has been worked for a long time by hand, assisted by a mallet and chisel. But things changed with the invention of dynamite, and later development saw the advent of motor-driven helicoid wire saws that could cut through the rock to transform them into blocks.

The motor rotated threads of iron wire that cut through the rock. A mixture of water and sand had to be added to the moving wires, the former to cool the metal, the latter to cut through the rock by means of abrasion. This technique continued to be used until the 1960s. Then came the development of the saws still in use today, which are a sort of diamond wire saw and work fundamentally in the same way. While they still cut by means of abrasion brought about by the artificial diamond coated rings located along the length of the cutting wires, there is no longer the need for water as a coolant. This equipment is faster and much more precise. As a result the role of the person whose job was to square off the rocks (which naturally split into irregular shapes) into geometric shapes was rendered superfluous.

Sentenced to death for being anarchists ... and Italian

Piazza Sacco e Vanzetti - 54033 Carrara (MS)
Piazza Sacco e Vanzetti is in front of the Carrara Hospital

Gn the side of the square facing the hospital is a small monument inaugurated on 23 August 2006 in memory of Nicola Sacco and Bartolommeo Vanzetti. Above their names are the two words *Gli Anarchici*, with the famous circled "A" that is the symbol of the anarchist movement. The ideas of the anarchists enjoy great support amongst the marble-workers, and the Sacco and Vanzetti affair caused a great stir in the region. The anarchist leader Antonio Meschi is also honoured here by a monument, in Piazza Gramsci.

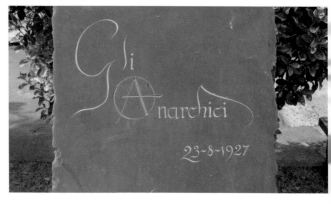

NEARBY
Michelangelo's column in the Nostra Signora del Sacro Cuore Oasis ㉓

502, Via Marconi - 55047 Seravezza (LU)
Tel: 0584 75 60 36

In 1519 Michelangelo was commissioned by Pope Leo X to design the façade of the church of San Lorenzo in Florence. In order to save money, the pontiff gave the contract for materials to the quarries of Seravazza instead of to those of Carrara. Thus Michelangelo went up to Mont Altissimo to supervise the work, getting directly involved in choosing each piece of marble and then setting to work on the columns (in spite of the fact that conditions were much more difficult than at Carrara because the quarry was further away from the coast). Once the columns were finished they were sent to Pisa, from where they were to be shipped up the river Arno to Florence. In a document dated 2 April

1519 (now in the Notarial Archives in Carrara), Michelangelo writes: "This Saturday I prepared the hooping of a large column, fifty braccia in length, before it was taken down to the coast. However, a link in the lewis broke and the column shattered into a hundred pieces in the river Serra.[...] We all risked getting killed, and we wasted a fine piece of marble...".

One part of that column was subsequently recovered and now stands in the Oasis Park. The plaque gives the date of its loss as early May – the only way in which it contradicts the account given in Michelangelo's letter.

But the story did not end there. Due to the delays resulting from having chosen the quarry at Seravezza, and the rising costs of the project, the façade of San Lorenzo was abandoned; it would, in fact, never be completed. Michelangelo had other equally important projects to work on, primarily the tomb of Julius II in Rome. Five of the twelve columns ordered are said to have been completed. Four of them were later rediscovered at the Teseco Foundation in Pisa. Only one of the columns ever reached Florence. Having been laid out in front of the church of San Lorenzo, it would wait in vain to be raised into place. The story goes that it was subsequently buried along the right side of the church, where some claim it still lies.

On 18 February 2007 laser lights were used to project onto the front of San Lorenzo a virtual image of the façade as it appears in Michelangelo's designs.

Sacco and Vanzetti

Nicola Sacco was born on 22 April 1892 at Torremaggiore in Puglia, and Bartolommeo Vanzetti in Vallifalletto (Piedmont) on 11 June 1888. After emigrating to the United States, they became separately involved with an Italo-American anarchist group, and both took refuge in Mexico to escape the draft (it was there they actually first met). Returning to Massachusetts, they would be accused of a hold-up during which two security guards were killed. After seven years of trials and appeals, they were executed in the electric chair on 23 August 1927, despite protests and the fact that a certain Madeiros had confessed to the crime. In reaction to the executions, veritable riots broke out in London, Paris, and various cities in Germany and Italy; even Benito Mussolini spoke up in the two men's defence. On 23 August 1977, exactly 50 years later, the governor of Massachusetts, Michael Dukakis, would clear their names. The Sacco and Vanzetti affair has inspired a large number of books and films, including Giuliano Montaldo's Sacco et Vanzetti. The most famous of the songs inspired by their story is Joan Baez's Here's to you, Nicola and Bart...

THE OLD CLEMENTI PHARMACY AND FACTORY

A little secret from the town of Fivizzano

Via Roma,111
Fivizzano (Province of Massa-Carrara)
Tel: 0585-92056 and 0585-926-864
Email: info@chinaclementi.it - www.chinaclementi.it

One of the town of Fivizzano's little secrets is its Clementi quinquina, which has been produced continuously by the family of the same name since 1884. It still follows the original recipe, created in the days when quinine was the only medicine available against fevers.

If you ask the owners of the establishment, who you will easily find in their historic pharmacy in Via Roma, they will happily let you visit (free of charge) the factory where the liqueur is produced. You will learn about the method by which this digestif is obtained and about the properties of its plant-based ingredients. This is one of the very rare quinquinas prepared from two distinct plants — red and yellow cinchona — just as prescribed by great-grandfather Giuseppe Clementi, a chemist and botanical expert.

NEARBY
The bas-relief of the Offiano pilgrim (25)

Offiano Parish Church
54014 Casola in Lunigiana (MS)
Directions: from Aulla take Road S63 towards Reggio Emilia. After 12 kms, turn right onto the S445. After Casola in Lunigiana, the sign to Offiano is a little further on, on the left.

Fitted into the left wall of the church at Offiano is a curious rectangle of white marble. Undoubtedly part of a bas-relief, it shows a pilgrim's scrip, feet and the lower part of his staff. Nowadays, of course, the place is well off the beaten track (to say the least), but this was even the case when pilgrims were travelling along the nearby Via Francigena, the old pilgrimage route which led from Canterbury, the mother church of English Christendom, to Rome and the tomb of St. Peter (see page 29). Despite this relative isolation, the church at Offiano – which is dedicated to St. Peter and appears in records dating back to 1148 – seems to have been a secondary object of interest to pilgrims, with the adjoining structure apparently being intended to provide accommodation for them.

CASTLE OF LA VERRUCOLA

The castle created by artists for the sake of art

Verrucola - Near Fivizzano (Province of Massa-Carrara)
Open: Fridays 1pm—5pm by appointment or by prior arrangement for visitors
with a particular interest in the works
Free entry — Donations gratefully accepted
Tel: (mob) 328-108-5576

The Castle of La Verrucola has dominated the medieval hamlet of the same name since the beginning of the 12th century.

This castle in the Lunigiana, 'the land of 100 castles', has undergone many changes since its construction and has been the victim of more than one earthquake. Its recent history from 1975 is of particular interest because that is when it was bought by the sculptor Pietro Cascella and his wife Cordelia von den Steinen, also a sculptor. She still lives there with their son Jacopo.

The couple's intervention has breathed new life into the old fortress. The Cascella family has transformed it into a true cultural workshop where artists from all over the world are made welcome. The rooms of the building are still used as a workshop by the family and their guests, although the death of Pietro Cascella in 2008 slowed this activity down. At the present time, the intention is to make it into a school of art with a connection to nature. Indeed, the castle enjoys a close symbiosis with nature.

Visitors currently have access to an impressive collection of works in the exciting castle armoury. This imposing room is vaulted and supported in the centre by a single octagonal pillar. It is certainly unusual. Many outline sculptures, mostly by Pietro, can be seen there. But there are also some of his completed works, along with works by his wife Cordelia and some pictures by their son Jacopo. A commentary by a close family member enhances the visit but visitors can also meet the artists in person. A private part of the collection on the upper floors can be viewed later.

Printing and publishing at Verrucola

Andreola dei Bosi, the mother of Pope Nicholas V who founded the Vatican Library, was a significant person who once lived in this village. It may be that the importance attached by her celebrated son to books also rubbed off on some of the other inhabitants of Verrucola and its surrounding area (Fivizzano). This could well explain what led Jacopo Onorati, better known as Jacopo da Fivizzano, to travel to Venice to learn the new art of printing.

On returning to his home town, Jacopo began producing printed books, quite some time before some other much better known European cities. It is thanks to him that the particular interest in printing and publishing characteristic of a large part of this region was propagated (see also the note on Montereggio p. 231).

Unfortunately the museum of printing at Fivizzano is closed, but it is possible to obtain information and request the town council to arrange a special opening via the following email: culturaeturismo@comune.fivizzano.ms.it. Or telephone 058-594-2175.

PARCO DEGLI AFFETTI

Italy's first pet cemetery

Brunella Nature Park
54011 Aulla (MS)
Park opening hours: in summer 8.30-19.30, 17.30 in winter. Closed on Monday

While there were already private burial areas for pets in Lombardy and Emilia Romagna*, the Aulla Parco degli Affetti is the first municipally-owned pet century in Italy; it is, however, run by a private company, not the town council. One must admit that this is a beautiful final resting-place for one's beloved pets, a very calm and serene spot commanding a fine westward view of the valley. Three thousand square metres have been given over to the cemetery and there are already around fifty tombs here, all in either wood or stone (the only materials allowed, for environmental reasons). For around 50 euros (local taxes included), you can acquire a plot, which is yours in perpetuity upon the payment of an annual maintenance charge. Suitable coffins can also be bought. The company running the cemetery can also collect a pet from anywhere in Italy and organise a cremation if that is preferred**.

For a pet burial, apply to :
Parco degli affetti. 22, Via Apua
54011 Aulla (MS)
Tel: 348 44 02 695 (Rita) or 0187 42 19 55

Directions: To reach the pet cemetery, enter the park laid out around the castle of La Brunella overlooking the town of Aulla, then go to the last car park near the top. The cemetery is laid out on the slope to the left of the footpath that leads up to the castle. Its entrance is marked by a totem depicting a cat and a dog.

---

* "Il Ponte dell'Arcobaleno" private pet cemetery at Villanova del Sillaro (LO), in Lombardy.
Tel: 328 76 94 905 and 320 72 46 070, www.pontedellarcobaleno.it/,
e-mail :info@pontedellarcobaleno.it
"Il paradiso di Tom & Jerry" private cemetery for large dogs (but also for hamsters and goldfish) at Altedo (BO),
29, Via Chiavicone. Tel: 0333 38 34 204 - www.ilparadisoditomejerry.com

** Dogs, cats and hamsters are accepted, but also 'two-legged' pets: canaries, parrots and other domestic birds.

THE CASTLE OF CASTIGLIONE DEL TERZIERE

The dream of a man, enlightenment of a people

Via del Borgo 1, Bagnone (Province of Massa-Carrara)
Open: Daily by request - Free admission
Tel: 018-742-9100 or 347-000-4486
Email: info@castellodicastiglionedelterziere.it
www.castellodicastiglionedelterziere.it

Beyond the hamlet, the manor house and village of Castiglione del Terziere reveal a project going back to 1969 when the oncologist, poet, humanist and dreamer Loris Jacopo Bononi bought the ruins.

By 1972 the new owner had restored this fine place to its former splendour. Then he set himself an even more ambitious mission: to transform the place into a beacon of civilisation, a perfect backdrop to reveal the area's culture and encourage awareness of it.

In recent times, the population of the Lunigiana has declined. In order to reinstate a sense of pride in its past amongst the younger generation, Bononi realised that it was necessary to encourage in them a feeling of belonging in this historic and renowned territory. So he searched around the world and brought back to Italy hundreds of works connected with the Lunigiana. As a result of his work we now have access to some of Jacopo de Fivizzano's early books, more than 5,000 first editions published in the region, sculptures by Bernini, and hundreds of other works of inestimable value. We are even encouraged to handle them because they are presented here without a pane of glass, a wall, or any other kind of non-physical barrier to prevent us doing so.

Visitors have free access to the castle, which is still inhabited. Mrs. Raffaella Paoletti, Loris Jacopo Bononi's partner, will act as your guide. She is now responsible for carrying on with the plan and pursuing the castle's mission, having contributed to it alongside her husband over the last thirty years.

The Lunigiana and its mysteries

The name Lunigiana derives from the Latin lunensis ager ("moon land"). Its centre was the ancient town of Luni, not far from the modern town of Sarzana (now in Liguria). Luni doubtless owes its name to the moon cult practised by those who lived in this region before the Romans. The cult was passed down in various forms until the Middle Ages. Evidence of it can be seen, for example, in the coat of arms of Fivizzano, which shows a bear's claw seizing a crescent moon.

FACION OR *FACCION* ON VILLAGE WALLS IN THE LUNIGIANA AREA

Faces of mysterious origin

Cervara
54027 Pontremoli (MS)

Around Pontremoli, a number of villages in the Lunigiana area contain houses whose walls are adorned with carved faces. Three of these are to be seen in the village of Cervara (in the village high street running parallel to the main road). Their origin is unknown, but there are those who say that they were carved to protect the inhabitants of the houses from the "Evil Eye."

NEARBY
Montereggio, book town ㉚
54026 Mulazzo (MS)

About 20 kilometres from Pontremoli is the small village of Montereggio di Mulazzo, a place which over the years has dedicated itself entirely to the book trade. Every resident here is a bookseller, with an open display of wares outside each house (trust reigns supreme). Though this tradition goes back some way, no one has yet explained how this village became a European distribution point for rare books and those which were banned elsewhere as subversive. In time, people from this village would open bookshops not only in Italy, but also in Spain and in Holland. Others would turn to publishing, founding some of Italy's best-known editorial houses. Furthermore, one of the country's most prestigious literary prizes – the Premio Bancarella [literally, "Bookstall Prize"] – is awarded at Pontremoli, another nearby "Book Town."

Livorno and surroundings

THE TONIETTI FAMILY MAUSOLEUM ①

The Tomb of the Mining Concession Holders

GTE, 57030 Cavo (LI)
*Directions: from the centre of Cavo go past the castle standing by the beach and
follow the one-way system that brings you back to the village by an inland route.
Leave the car at the car park just before the back of the castle and then take the
GTE (Grande Traversata d'Elba), a wide footpath that starts on the right of the
car park and goes towards Monte Grosso. Allow a good twenty minutes to get to
the mausoleum up a moderate incline*

T his Art Nouveau mausoleum was designed by the architect Adolfo Coppedè (1871-1951), whose brother Gino (1866-1927) would lend his name to an entire district of Rome (around Via Dora). Looking like a lighthouse seen from the sea, the monument is built of both local and Carrara marble. Above the entrance is the inscription "Famiglia Tonetti" under a seagull with outstretched wings (some say the bird depicted is an eagle). Very neglected, the mausoleum is in a poor state, and the interior, which contains four tomb openings, is covered in graffiti.

An eminent member of a family native to Elba, Giuseppe Tonietti would become the concession holder of the Elba iron mines in 1888. After his death in 1894, he was succeeded by his son Ugo Ubaldo Tonietti. Together with the director of the mining company, Pilade del Buono, the son would form a very enterprising partnership, establishing a blast-furnace plant at Portoferraio so that the iron ore mined on the island could be smelted locally. At the beginning of the 20th century the Tonietti family fortunes were at their high point. It was then that Ugo Ubaldo decided to have this mausoleum built at Cavo. Work on the monument began in 1904 and was completed two years later. It would never be used as a tomb because the family did not obtain permission for a private burial place.

NEARBY

An "Iron Cross" of Pyrites ②

Alfeo Ricci Mineralogy Museum
Via Palestro 57031 Capoliveri (LI)
Tel: 0565 93 54 92
Opening hours: from April to October, daily 10.00-13.00 and 16.30-18.30
Admission: 2.50 €, reduced: 1.50 €

The Elba Mineralogy Museum houses the important collection of minerals gathered together by its founder, Alfeo Ricci. One unusual piece is a double pentadodecahedron – that is, a sixty-sided piece – of iron pyrites in the form of an 'iron cross'. Composed primarily of sulphur and iron, pyrites is very common on Elba. It owes its name to the Greek for fire (pyros): when it is struck against iron, it sparks. The rarity of this particular piece is that the two crystals within the pyrites have grown across each other to form this strange motif of the "iron cross".

CASA SALDARINI

A house in the shape of a mushroom

Villini 1 Car Park
The Archaeological Park of Baratti and Populonia
Baratti
57025 Piombino (LI)

This abandoned house in the middle of the Archaeology Park seems to have been entirely forgotten about ever since its construction in 1962 for the Saldarini family. Designed by the architect Vittorio Giorgini, it was inspired by the idea that architectural forms should echo those of the natural world and therefore fit in with the natural environment.

This house was a first in Italy for both method of construction and the materials used. There were those who criticised it at the time as kitsch, as nothing but a piece of sculpture, or as a house without form. The nicknames given to the building – the "tortoise", the "elephant", etc – reveal the attempts made to identify the daring design with something familiar and obvious. A little too avant-garde for its day, the house found no new buyer after the Saldarini family moved in the 1980s.

Another building by Vittorio Girogini stands not far away: the wood-built holiday home called L'Esagono [the Hexagon]. This is visible, from the outside only, if you take the path to the right that runs around Casa Saldarini. The concept behind this structure was modular, given that it consists of prefabricated hexagonal components (like those that make up a beehive), which were then fitted together and organised in accordance with the owner's requirements.

Vittorio Giorgini

Born in Florence in 1926, Vittorio Giorgini began teaching architecture in the United States in 1969. Most of the models and plans of the designs by this very atypical architect are now to be found in France (at the Centre Pompidou in Paris and the FRAC in Orléans) or in Switzerland (at the Vita Design Museum, Basle). Giorgini's works in Tuscany also include a school in Bibbona. Author of a number of books, the architect is known for his iconoclastic ideas. One of his works is available on-line for consultation at: www.bibliotecamarxista.org/autori/giorgini%20vittorio.htm

His architectural work is discussed in Marco Del Francia's Vittorio Giorgini, la natura come modello published by Edizioni Angelo Pontecorboli in 2000.

Directions: there are no signs indicating the Casa Saldarini. Take the SP23 which links San Vincenzo and Piombino and then follow the arrows to the Baratti and Populonia Archaeological Park. Turn right into the first car park (Villini 1) and leave your car at the end of the road, in the area of the bars and restaurants. Then take the beaten-earth track that starts to the left of the Demos restaurant, and walk for around one hundred metres. Casa Saldarini is within a walled garden and the gate is locked. The building is now abandoned and the garden overgrown (obstructing the view to the sea). Unfortunately it is not possible to visit the interior.

THE MYSTERIES OF CAMPIGLIA

Perfect for lovers of the esoteric

Church of San Giovanni – Municipal Cemetery. Via di Venturina
57021 Campiglia Marittima (LI)
Cemetery opening hours: from 1 May to 30 September 7.30-18.00 (Mondays and
Fridays 17.00-18.00); 1 October to 30 April 8.00-17.00 (Mondays and Fridays
from 14.00-17.00)
"House of Alchemy". 4 Via B. Buozzi . 57021 Campiglia Marittima (LI)

F or lovers of the esoteric, the village of Campiglia Marittima is a little paradise; the streets in the village and the area around the church of San Giovanni are full of mysterious symbols and details.

The church walls have been roped off to prevent visitors getting too close, so you need binoculars to read a plaque with a palindrome identical to one that can be found in Siena:

SATOR

AREPO

TENET

OPERA

ROTAS

For the explanation, see the chapter on Siena (page 79).

A few metres away, the ground in front of the church door is paved with what was undoubtedly a tombstone. This bears various inscriptions - including one which reads Tolomeus Petri et Flore – and a very curious central motif: an androgynous body which is male below the waist, female above (the figure seems to be holding a torch in its right hand, while supporting itself against some sort of slanting board). Strangely, this same figure reappears on the house at number 4 Via B. Buozzi in the village. There it is more distinct and one can make out details that are not so clear on the church flagstone: for example, the figure's right hand no longer seems to be holding a torch but rather the number '3'. Surrounding the image one sees a number of esoteric symbols, which have inevitably led some to argue that this is a "House of Philosophy" associated with alchemy. Unfortunately there is no real explanation as to who the "philosopher" in question might be ... just as there is no explanation for the air of mystery with which the village seems to both excite and defeat curiosity.

Note: you have to walk through the cemetery to reach the church. The gate locks automatically at closing time (further adding to the air of mystery here). Thus you are strongly advised to respect the opening times if you do not want to end up locked in the cemetery overnight...

THE TRIPLE ENCLOSURE OF SAN SILVESTRO CATHEDRAL

Traditional game or esoteric symbol ?

San Silvestro Park of Archaeology and Mining
34b, Via di San Vincenzo. 57021 Campiglia Marittima (LI)
Tel: 0565 83 86 80
Guided tours and bookings: 0565 22 64 45
E-Mail: parcoss@parchivaldicornia.it - www.parchivaldicornia.it
Opening times: from June to September, Tuesday to Sunday; in July and August, daily; and from March to May, Saturdays, Sundays, and holidays. In winter you are advised to phone ahead to confirm. The park opens at 10am, and closes at different times according to the season of the year. Admission to the park, with all the various facilities (little train, museums, commentaries): 9 €, reduced: 5 €
The San Silvestro Citadel - the Rocca di San Silvestro – can be reached either on foot (a forty minute walk) or by means of the small train that carries guided tours and leaves at set times (every hour during high season)

The Citadel of San Silvestro dates from the year 1004. Near the fortified main gate is a curious motif carved into the stone (now protected by a glass panel). Not far away, another identical motif can be found on the third step of the entrance staircase; it is not signposted. A panel at the main way explains that the carving depicts the game of filetto [Nine Men's Morris] which was played by the guards here during the long hours when they were on watch.

Also known as "Merels", Nine Men's Morris is known to have been played in ancient Egypt, Greece and Rome. The motif of the morris board can be found in England (Whitby Abbey, Westminster Abbey, Canterbury Cathedral), in France (the Abbey of Chaalis, Oise) and at innumerable places in Italy: the castle of Campolattaro (Benevento, Campania), the basilica of St. John Lateran (Rome), the church of San Francesco in Alatri (outside Frosinone, Latium) and the church of San Rocco (Venice) ... to name but a few. The game was played on a board of three concentric squares; the centres of each side linked by a line, with diagonals also running from the corner of the inner square out to the corner of the outer. The resulting junctions of lines and square form the 24 places where the two players could, one at a time, put down their nine men (or pawns). The aim was to form a full line of three whilst preventing your opponent from doing the same. Sometimes the pieces were simply different-coloured pebbles.

Some have argued against this interpretation of the motif, saying that it actually depicts the esoteric symbol of the "triple enclosure"; the citadel of San Silvestro itself is in part contained within triple rings of ramparts. To support their theory they point out that the diagram is vertical, and therefore could not have been used to play Nine Men's Morris. Various explanations of the triple enclosure have been put forward. Some have said it is a ground plan of the city of Poseidon, the capital of Atlantis, some that it is a representation of the Temple of Jerusalem contained within its triple walls, and still others that it is a diagrammatic depiction of an alchemical "squaring of the circle."

Another game board was found during excavations at the citadel. This was used for the game of alquerque (el qirkat), which the Arabs had introduced into Spain some time around the 10th century.

PETRA AZIENDA AGRICOLA

A monument to architecture in the middle of the countryside

131, San Lorenzo Alto - 57038 Suvereto (LI)
Tel: 0565 84 53 08
E-mail: info@petrawine.it
www.petrawine.it
Visits and wine-tasting by appointment only

The first thought that comes to mind when you get to the Petra winery is that you have taken a wrong turn somewhere. It's easy to imagine that this spectacular building is a Futurist monument commemorating some extraordinary event., But much more prosaically, it is in fact the premises of the vineyards run by the father and daughter team of Vittorio and Francesca Moretti, who commissioned renowned architect Mario Botta to design the structure. The property covers some 300 hectares of vineyards, woods and olive groves, producing four different ranges of wines and olive oil (sold in a bottle also of very unusual design).

Mario Botta

Born on 1 April 1943 at Mendrisio (in the Swiss canton of Ticino), Mario Botta is undoubtedly a leading figure in contemporary architecture. Having joined an architectural studio as a junior draughtsman at the age of 15, he would design his first building a year later: the presbytery at Genetrerio (Ticino). He would then take up his studies again and open his own studio in 1970 in Lugano. Since then he has produced work that exemplifies a personal style which he describes as embodying a "regressive utopia", and a "refuge centred once more upon tradition." His buildings show a marked preference for the use of brick, with designs often employing a keystone motif along with a massive central cylinder. His most famous projects include the cathedral at ñvry (France), the San Francisco Museum of Modern Art (USA), the Gotardo Bank (Lugano, Switzerland), the extension and modernisation of La Scala Opera House in Milan (Italy) and, most famous of all, the "Round House" at Stabio (Switzerland).

NEARBY

Statue of Carducci's grandmother ⑦

Piazza Alberto. Bolgheri - 57022 Castagneto Carducci (LI)

Alhough there is no sign recording the fact, the model for the statue of the old lady calmly sitting on a bench in the central square of this fine little village was in fact the grandmother of the Italian poet Giosuè Carducci. His beloved "Nonna Lucia" had a decisive influence on his early years, even though she died when he was seven years old. She is mentioned in a number of his works, most notably in Davanti San Guido. Born on 27 July 1835, Giosuè Carducci lived in Bolgheri until 1848 (his father was a doctor here). The poet would ultimately win the Nobel Prize for Literature in 1906, though he was too ill at the time to go and receive the award. He died on 16 February 1907 in Bologna.

THE MADONNA OF FRASSINE

A miraculous Madonna on a tree-trunk

The Frassine Sanctuary - 58020 Frassine (GR)
Tel: 0566 91 00 00
www.santuariomadonnadelfrassine.com
Opening hours: daily, 8.45-12.00 and 14.00-17.00

Standing in an illuminated niche above the high altar, the miraculous statue of the Madonna is immediately visible when you enter the church of the Sanctuary of Frassine. Access behind the altar is via the iron gates on either side (ask the priest or sacristan). Once there, you discover the apse of the small original chapel that has been incorporated within this larger church. Upon opening the door to the right of the apse you are greeted by an amazing sight: the tall trunk of an ash tree on which the statue of the Virgin stands.

In the 6th century St. Regulus, having fled Africa because of the persecution of the Christians, landed with several of his disciples at Baratta. All the saint brought with him was a cedar-wood statue of the Virgin, which would be preserved by the monks of the monastery of San Pietro near Monteverdi Marritimo after Regulus was beheaded by order of Totila, king of the Ostrogoths.

In the 13th century the monastery was sacked and destroyed. However, a monk by the name of Mariano managed to carry the statue

to safety, hiding it within the branches of an ash tree. One century later, a herdsman was made curious by the fact that his animals always knelt down at one precise spot in the forest. Upon investigation, he found the statue, resting upon the trunk of the tree as upon a high pedestal. The statue was then carried to a local church, only to later return in some inexplicable manner to its place in the tree. Understanding the significance of this return, the local people built a chapel around the statue, and the sanctuary of Frassine subsequently became the site of numerous miracles.

EX-VOTOS AT THE SANCTUARY OF THE MADONNA OF MONTENERO

An ex-voto that inspired the plot of Rossini's opera, L'Italiana in Algeri

57128 Livorno (LI)
Tel: 0586 57 771
E-Mail: info@santuariomontenero.org
www.santuariomontenero.org
Opening hours: Sundays and holidays 7.00-13.00 and 14.30-18.00; weekdays 7.30-12.30 and 14.30-18.30

Located in a spot overlooking Livorno and the surrounding area, the sanctuary of Montenero was built in 1721 on the site of a miracle. It contains a large number of ex-votos, most of them for grace received at sea. Alongside the naïve but moving paintings of shipwrecks and storms, there are also works of exceptional artistic quality, making the ex-votos here into a veritable museum collection of seascapes. However, the ex-votos are not always paintings. For example, there is the bloody undervest of a policeman (left in 1935), or the waistcoat and oriental slippers of a young woman from Ponsivinio who, around the year 1800, was seized by Turkish pirates while out strolling along the beach of Antignano. Taken to Constantinople, she was forced to enter the Sultan's harem. Then one day her incessant prayers to the Virgin were answered: there in the harem's garden she saw her own brother, who, with the Virgin's help, had come to rescue her. When she arrived back home, she had her Turkish clothes framed and then took them as an ex-voto to the Montenero sanctuary, where they can still be seen today.

Some say that it was this ex-voto which suggested the plot of Rossini's *L'Italiana in Algeri*, whilst others argue the story was based upon the misfortunes which befell the Milanese gentlewoman Antonietta Frapolli: captured by pirates, she was taken to Algiers and forced to become part of the harem of the Bey, but would eventually be brought back to Italy by a Venetian ship.

The church also has other "Islamic" ex-votos: to thank the Madonna of Montenero for the intercession which spared him the amputation of a wounded leg, the son of the Bey of Tunis sent the sanctuary a model of that same limb in solid silver.

Ex-votos

The term "ex-voto" is an abbreviated form of the Latin *ex voto suscepto*, meaning "by reason of the vow made". These are tokens of gratitude offered to a saint (or the Virgin Mary) after a "miracle" has occurred, very often involving survival of shipwreck, accident, or illness. When a saint has answered the prayers of the faithful, the ex-voto offered can take either the form of an object (such as a crutch or a lifebuoy) or, more often, a naïve but descriptive painting of the incident involved. Sometimes ex-votos can even be anthropomorphic (see page 101 in connection with the sanctuary of Romituzzo).

THE ENGLISH CEMETERY IN LIVORNO

Italy's oldest Protestant cemetery

Misericordia di Livorno, 63, Via Giuseppe Verdi - 57126 Livorno (LI)
Tel: 0586 89 73 24
Ask for the keys at the office of the Misericordia di Livorno
Opening hours: Monday to Thursday 9.00-12.00 and 14.00-17.00, Friday 9.00-12.00

The English cemetery of Livorno is a very unexpected and secluded spot in the centre of the city. Visited by scholars, curious English tourists, and those devoted to St. Elizabeth Seaton (see below), it is a charming place where the shrubs and plants have gradually reasserted their rights, in some cases overturning the tombstones. Amidst birdsong, buzzing insects, and occasionally, the strident sound of televisions in the nearby apartment blocks, one has to step carefully to avoid tripping over the overgrown stones that litter the ground. Sometimes the eye is caught by a Swiss tombstone, for although this place is referred to as the "English Cemetery", it was used by all those of Protestant faith, irrespective of nationality. However, it is the United Kingdom which, via its Consulate in Florence, remains responsible for this "little corner of Britain." Until 1827, when the Swiss Reformed Church opened an ecumenical cemetery in Florence, all foreigners who died in Italy and were neither Catholic nor Jewish could only be buried here at Livorno (or Leghorn, as the English called it at the time).

The dates on the tombstones reveal a curious paradox: the cemetery was in use long before it was officially recognised. In fact, that official recognition only came in 1746, while the oldest tombstone here dates back to 1594. The cemetery would remain in use until 1839, when a new one was opened near the city's San Marco gate. Protected by a sheet of glass, the most frequently visited tomb here is that of William Magee Seaton, husband of St. Elizabeth Seaton, who was herself converted to Catholicism while living in Livorno. Paul Valéry compared the English cemetery in Livorno to a sculptor's studio.

Saint Elizabeth Ann Seaton

Born in New York City on 28 August 1774 into a Protestant family, Ann Bayley would marry William Magee Seaton in 1794. After her husband went bankrupt and then fell ill with TB, the family travelled to Livorno in the hope that the sea air might provide a cure. However, William faded fast and would be buried in the English cemetery.

Elisabeth, by now a convert to Catholicism, returned to the USA with her five children and became a teacher. She would open a school for young girls in Maryland, then a religious community – the Sisters of Charity – in Baltimore. She died on 4 January 1821 and was canonised on 14 September 1975 by Pope Paul VI. She was the first woman in the United States to be declared a saint.

NEARBY

The marble bridge ⑪

The bridge which links Via Borra and Via Porticciolo owes its name to the marble edging on which numerous boatmen and porters have, over the decades, engraved names and inscriptions. These commemorations of dead friends, sometimes referred to solely by their surname, are often very moving. For example, one reads: "To the dear memory of Giovanni Calafatti who ceased to enjoy the gentle breeze of life on 16 September 1854, at the age of 26, being carried off by an evil sickness. His friends in condolence for such a loss had this marble carved. P.P. [Pregate per Lui. Pray for Him]"

Ruins of the mausoleum of Costanzo Ciano ⑫
Monte Burrone - 57128 Livorno (LI)

The mausoleum can be reached by car or on foot (600 metres from the car park). From the car park for the Montenero sanctuary, take Via Giovanni XXIII and then turn left into the first unsurfaced road, Viale Tirreno.

At the top of Monte Burrone stands a massive square tower now heavily tagged by graffiti artists and in the process of being reclaimed by nature. This is all that is left of the unfinished mausoleum of Costanzo Ciano, father of Galeazzo Ciano, who was Benito Mussolini's son-in-law (husband of his daughter Edda) and Foreign Minister in the Fascist government. Famous for a feat of arms carried out in 1918 – by boat, he managed to penetrate 80 km behind the Austrian defences at Buccari in Croatia – Costanzo Ciano was honoured by Mussolini with this monumental mausoleum, designed by the architect Arturo Dazzi, a personal friend of Galeazzo Ciano. But dismayed by his country's adverse fortunes during the Second World War, Galeazzo attempted to negotiate a separate peace for Italy with the Allies in 1943. Arrested by the Nazis, he was handed over to Mussolini, who had him shot on 11 January 1944... Hence the mausoleum to his father was never finished...

The first apartment blocks in Italy ⑬
Venezia Nuova District

Begun in the 17th century, work on the New Venice district produced Italy's first apartment blocks. These collective residential buildings, with different apartments on different floors, were intended to provide those who worked at sea with functional accommodation near the port. Most of the structures were destroyed by Allied bombing in 1944, but they were later rebuilt exactly as they had been.

Palazzo Gaudi

(14)

Via della Repubblica - 57013 Rosignano Solvay (LI)

Loosely inspired by the style of Gaudi, this building proudly asserts its links with that architect's work. Designed by Veronica Cantina, it has provoked very varied reactions amongst the inhabitants of Rosignano. The structure certainly stands out amidst the usual urban fabric and all of its apartments were quickly sold, confirming the success of this original project. The architect dedicated one of the main entrance towers to the Sun and the other to the Moon.

Piazza della Repubblica – The Widest Bridge in Europe
Built in 1844 to join the old and new districts of the city, Piazza della Repubblica is in effect a bridge spanning the city's main canal, the Fosse Reale. 240 metres in width, it is therefore – as the guidebooks point out – the widest bridge in Europe.

Grosseto and surroundings

THE TOMB OF TIBURZI, THE "BANDIT KING"

Lower limbs buried inside the walls, upper limbs outside...

Capalbio Cemetery
Via Giacomo Leopardi
58011 Capalbio (GR)

In the period immediately before the Unification of Italy the poorest peasants survived only thanks to such time-honoured rights as riverside fishing, the collection of windfall timber and the gleaning of cornfields. The abolition of these rights meant penury for hundreds, with some being forced to become bandits and outlaws if they were not to starve. Domenico Tiburzi, known as Domenichino, was one such. Born at Cellere (outside Viterbo) on 26 May 1836, he was the most famous of all the bandits in the area, actually being nicknamed "The King of Maremma". He drew a distinction between justice and the written law, and owed his popularity to his observance of a personal moral code: for example, he robbed from the rich to give to the poor, and once killed a fellow bandit who was "doing wrong." But he was also accused of working as "'muscle'" for a number of rich landowners, carrying out well-paid "contracts" that were not inspired by any fine sense of justice.

Eventually, in 1896, Tiburzi was ambushed and shot by the carabinieri, just outside Capalbio; the famous picture of the bandit leaning against a column in the Capalbio cemetery is actually a photograph of his dead body held in place by ropes. Initially, the Church refused to accede to the popular demand that the bandit be given a religious burial. Finally, a compromise was reached and Tiburzi was buried under the very wall of the cemetery, with this lower limbs reaching into sacred ground, but the upper part of his body lying outside. Today there is no gravestone to mark the tomb; but one can still see the column that appears in the famous photograph. A small wooden panel recalls the date and place of Tiburzi's death.

If you want to know more, go to the Trattoria Da Maria in the village, where there is an exhibit of newspaper articles and other documents dealing with the life and beaux gestes of Domenico Tiburzi.
Trattoria Da Maria, 3 Via Comunale - 58011 Capalbio (GR). Tel: 0564 89 60 14. Closed Tuesdays and from 7 January to 10 February. Tiburzi, Paolo Benvenuti's film about the bandit, came out in 1996.

For lovers of stories of brigands and bandits, there is also the opportunity to sleep in the house that once belonged to the famous bandit Antonio Magrini, nicknamed "Il Basilocco'". The last great brigand of the Maremma, he was killed by the carabinieri in 1904. The weapons he had with him at his death – a pistol, a rifle and a dagger – have been preserved.
Fattoria di Peruzzo 58028 Roccatederighi (GR). Tel: 0564 56 98 73. E-mail: info@peruzzofattoria.com. www.peruzzofattoria.com. From 420? to 670? per week.

THE "CUT"

A spectacular Roman canal cut into the rock

Ansedonia, 58010 Orbetello (GR)
Directions: Travelling southbound on the Via Aurelia, take the second exit (Ansedonia); travelling northbound it's the first exit. The road then takes you directly to the promontory

L a Tagliata [The Cut] is a spectacular piece of Roman engineering dating from the 2nd century BC. Slicing through an 80-metre stretch of rock that is at times 20 metres deep, the canal was cut to link the Etruscan port of Cosa with the lake of Burano; it also served as a

means of tidal control to prevent the port from silting up. Today, La Tagliata is freely open to visitors, a few minor adjustments having been made so that the entire site is accessible.

The Torre della Tagliata is a tower that was subsequently converted into a house. One famous resident was Giacomo Puccini, who lived here while working on Turandot, the opera he left unfinished at his death.

NEARBY

Transatlantic hydroplane flights from Orbetello air base

Parco delle Crociere. 1-7, Via Marconi, 58010 Orbetello (GR)
The monument is protected by a gate, but those in charge are quite happy to open it for visitors. If no one is around, contact: Air Force Captain Romualdi: 329 36 08 085, Mr. Giusti Alfredo: 0564 86 76 13, Command Post, Air Force Deposit 64b, Porto Santo Stefano: 0564 81 68 02

The Parco delle Crociere stands on the site of the Orbetello Air Base, destroyed by the Germans in 1944. A monument recalls that this airfield was the starting-point for a number of legendary flights, two of them undertaken by Italo Balbo (see below). What was so spectacular about these flights was that they involved a large number of hydroplanes and covered distances that were remarkable for the time. The first of these took place in 1928, with more than 60 hydroplanes crossing the western Mediterranean, from Orbetello to Los Alcazares in Spain. Italo Balbo would later pilot two transatlantic flights – to Rio de Janeiro (1930) and New York and Chicago (1933). These flights attracted huge international media coverage, promoting a very positive and modern image of Italy.

Italo Balbo

Italo Balbo was born near Ferrara on 6 June 1896. Although the son of a bourgeois family which supported the monarchy, as a young man he made his political commitment to republican ideas known. After earning medals and promotion to the rank of captain during the First World War, Balbo became a member of the Fascist movement, and was one of the four main figures in the "March on Rome" in 1922. Quick to brawl with Communists and Socialists, he was even accused of the murder of an anti-Fascist priest. But the Ferrara court which reheard the case in 1947, after the collapse of Fascism, would exonerate him.

Balbo's passion for flying led to his appointment as Minister of Aviation at the age of 33, making him the youngest government minister in Europe. It was while he held that position that he would undertake his two famous transatlantic flights (see above). His fame was then at its height: streets in America were named after him; New York gave him a ticker-tape parade; the Sioux named him "Chief Flying Eagle" and in common parlance the word "balbo" was used to refer to a fleet of aircraft.

Becoming Governor of Libya in 1934, he would initiate various grandiose projects, including the coastal road that became known as Via Balbia. In 1939, the Nazi invasion of Poland brought to a head the decline in his relationship with Mussolini, whom he criticised for his alliance with the Germans and for the promulgation of the Race Laws. On 28 June 1940, Balbo's plane was shot down by Italian anti-aircraft guns when he was returning from a reconnaissance flight over Tobruk. Certain people, including his widow, cast doubt on the official version of events, claiming he had been murdered on Mussolini's orders. In fact, Mussolini himself once said that Balbo was the only man he feared, because he thought that Balbo alone was capable of assassinating him.

The day after Balbo's death, a Royal Air Force plane piloted by Raymond Collishaw, a Canadian air ace during the First World War, flew over the Italian military camp to drop a wreath with a sash expressing the RAF's condolences. Along with those of his crew members, Italo Balbo's tomb can be seen in the Orbetello cemetery, in Viale Donatori del Sangue.

STATUE OF CARAVAGGIO

Beneath the sands of La Feniglia lies the body of Caravaggio...

Braccio Car Park
La Feniglia Beach, Porto Ercole
58019 Monte Argentario (GR)
Parking: 1 € an hour

Among the various aspects of Caravaggio's life that are shrouded in mystery, his birth and death continue to puzzle scholars. While we know that the painter – real name, Michelangelo Merisi – was born on 29 September 1571, it has yet to be established with certainty that his birthplace actually was Caravaggio, just outside Bergamo. Some biographers argue that he was born in Milan and that he then spent part of his childhood in the village which would give him his artistic name. As for his death, it raises a number of unanswered questions. We know that the artist was sentenced to death for having killed a certain Ranuccio Tommasoni in a duel. As a result he was forced to live outside Rome. Later, after hearing that the Pope was going to grant him a pardon, he tried to return to the city by sea. However, when his ship put in at Porto Ercole (or, as some argue, Palo, near the Etruscan necropolis of Cerveteri), he is said to have been arrested by customs officers but then released upon payment of a ransom. By the time he got free, the boat carrying his baggage and paintings he intended to present to the Pope had left port. And in his frantic efforts to beat it to its next port of call, Caravaggio is said to have caught a fever on the deserted beach of La Feniglia, dying on 18 July 1610. But there are also those who claim that he was the victim of a hired killer…

While his actual burial place has never been found, in 2001 scholars did unearth the record of his death in the parish register of the church of Sant-Erasmo in Porto Ercole. Ironically, the artist died without knowing that the Pope had put his seal to the act of pardon…

Note: this is the site of a kind of vague copy of Caravaggio's famous *Medusa* in the Uffizi Gallery in Florence.

After Orbetello carry on towards Porto Ercole then turn left towards Ansedonia. Turn left again at the sign *"Parking, Noleggio bici, Spiaggia libera"* — "Parking, Bike hire, Public beach". The path to this attraction is not signposted.

It is best to park your car in the Braccio car park (there is a charge). Leave the car park on foot on the side opposite the entrance and follow a long path until you see a milestone marking kilometre zero for the direction you are walking and kilometre six for the opposite direction. Take the path just to the left — it isn't marked but is clearly visible and takes you through the pine wood to another wide-laid path parallel to the first. Turn left onto this path and after another hundred metres or so you will see the attraction.

If you have any concerns about finding your way, try communicating using wild gesticulations; the car park cashier will explain how to get there. Many senior citizens also roam about here on bicycles and will no doubt happily furnish you with any directions you need.

MOSAICS IN THE CHURCH OF SANTISSIMA TRINITÀ

The "Two Europes" joined under the Trinity

Via Ss Trinità
Pozzarello
Porto Santo Stefano
58019 Monte Argentario (GR)

The church of Santa Trinità was consecrated in 2002. The first thing that strikes you upon entering is the large mosaic covering the apse wall behind the high altar. These aesthetically daring motifs and colours are unusual, even for a modern church, and are the work of a team from the Ezio Aletti Centro Studi e Ricerche.

With its head office in Rome, the Aletti Centre was set up by the Jesuits to further mutual understanding between the "two Europes" that are in the process of political unification. Specialists in the culture and religion of central and eastern Europe, members of the Centre work to promote cultural exchange and cooperation. While spiritual questions are an essential concern for the centre, it also collaborates in the decoration of new places of worship, drawing upon such traditional artistic crafts as mosaics.

The work in the church of Santa Trinità depicts the Holy Trinity, with the hand of God the Father above and the dove which symbolises the Holy Spirit. Below is the third member of the Trinity, Jesus, who reaches out towards Adam and Eve. The figure of the pelican was a traditional symbol of sacrifice: it was once believed that the bird pecked its chest so that its offspring could drink its blood.

Centro Studi e Ricerche Ezio Aletti
25, Via Paolina. 00184 Rome
Tel: 06 48 24 588
www.centroaletti.com
Pozarello lies between Orbetello and Porto Santo Stefano. The road up to the church (Via Ss Trinità) runs off the main street. The church bell-tower provides a clear visual landmark.

THE MADONNA OF THE CAT FLAP ⑥

A 15th century painting... complete with cat flap

Church of San Giorgio
Piazza San Giorgio
58014 Montemerano (GR)

The church of San Giorgio at Montemerano is known best for a polyptych by Sano di Pietro (1406-1481), The Madonna and Child with Saints. But to the right of the high altar is another painting that is worthy of attention. Now known as "La Madonna della gattaiola" [Madonna of the Cat Flap], this wood panel was painted around 1450 by a pupil of Sassetta's (1392-1451) who would become known as Il Maestro di Montemerano.

Originally, it was part of a diptych of The Annunciation. However, when the door to the cellar in the presbytery broke, the parish priest decided to replace it with this panel, which happened to be the same size. The problem was that he kept salami, cheese and fruit in his cellar, so he needed a cat down there to keep off the rats and mice. To make it possible for this feline guard to come and go, he had a round hole cut in the panel. It is still there, perfectly visible, and has given the work its present nickname.

NEARBY

A rare image of the legendary Baphomet ⑦
Parish Church of Santa Cristina, Ospedaletto. 10, Viccolo III° Borgo.
Rocchette di Fazio. 58055 Semproniano (GR)

The Templars' Cross on the pediment of the parish church of Santa Cristina at Rocccchette di Fazio probably indicates that the church was once connected with the Knights Templar. Some claim that one of the knights is buried in the crypt, along with his horse, sword, and substantial treasure. Just alongside the church is the Ospedaletto, a small hospice for the pilgrims which dates from the 14th century: High up on the left side wall is a sculpture which is supposed to be a depiction of the legendary Baphomet, a figure who played a key role in the destruction of the Order of the Knights Templar.

Baphomet

The *Baphomet* is an idol which is sometimes depicted with two or three faces (generally bearded), and sometimes takes a more animal form. During their trial, the Knights Templar were accused of bowing in veneration before an image of Baphomet during their initiation rituals; hence the accusation of heresy levelled against them. Various theories have been put forward as to the origin of the name, one pointing out that in the langue d'oc spoken in southern France "Baphomet" is the distorted version of "Mohammed".

THE TOWER OF DAVID

The tower of a 19th century "prophet"

Monte Labro
58031 Arcidosso (GR
Directions: Leave Arcidosso by the Strada del Monte Amiata (the SP 160). About 6km in the direction of Triana, there is a sign on the right to Monte Labro. Take this road, which after 3km brings you to a car park and a small chalet for visitors (open during the tourist season). Allow a good 15 minutes for the walk to the top of the hill

*G*iurisdavidism was a 19th century movement named after its founder, David Lazzaretti. In 1868 he and his disciples raised this tower on an area of bare rock exposed to the elements; the wind here can sometimes be very strong. The view from the top of the tower (altitude: 1,193m) is quite simply exceptional. The entrance to the tower itself

is in the unusual form of an inverted "V". If you have brought a torch with you, it is also possible to explore the underground area, whose entrance is immediately below the tower; the grill is closed only to keep out animals. Once inside, you can see the (now empty) chapel where the faithful used to meet. The Centro Studi Lazzaretti in Arcidosso has various mementoes of Lazzaretti's life as well as all the documentation relating to Giurisdavidism, a utopian socio-religious movement.

David Lazaretti

Born in Arcidosso in 1834, David Lazzaretto had his first visions when suffering from an attack of malaria. The young man then abandoned his wife and children to join the army. Having returned, he was one day at the top of Monte Labro when the Virgin appeared to him, announcing that he was descended from the House of Capet and that he had an evangelical mission to fulfil. Opinion varies as to whether the man was a prophet, a magus, or the leader of a sect. What is true is that his "New Zion" attracted an increasing number of followers. Preaching a sort of utopian-mystical socialism, Davide Lazzaretti would fall foul of the Catholic Church, which excommunicated him and forbade him all religious office. The authorities, too, took an increasingly repressive attitude and Lazzaretti himself would be shot dead by the police in Arcidosso while leading a demonstration on 18 August 1878. His body would later be exhumed and handed over to the (in)famous anthropologist Cesare Lombroso, the founder of morphopsychology and advocate of the theory of the "born criminal".

Centro Studi Lazzaretti
30, Piazza Indipendenza, 58031 Arcidosso (GR)
Tel: 0564 966438
E-mail biblioteca@amiata.net
www.centrostudilazzaretti.it

THE CROSSES OF BALDASSARE AUDIBERT

(9)

« He eats, drinks, carouses and raises crosses at all four corners »

Around Castel del Piano (GR)

At the middle of the 19th century a very strange fellow came to live in Castel del Piano. Was Baldassare Audibert, a guest of the owners of Palazzo Ginanneschi (today the Town Hall), actually a French bishop, a Belgian-born officer in Napoleon's armies, or simply a Frenchman from Vercelli in Piedmont?

What we do know is that, after a pilgrimage to Rome, he began raising crosses all over the locality of Castel del Piano, saying that he did so as an act of penitence for the fact that, as a member of the Convention during the French Revolution, he had voted for the execution of both Louis XVI and Marie-Antoinette.

The local people do not seem to have taken him that seriously, as one can see from this mocking verse:

Baldassarre Audiberte
Mangia beve e si diverte
Pianta croci alli cantoni
*Alla barba dei coglioni**

Sixteen of these crosses can now be seen in Castel del Piano and the neighbouring towns. Some were restored recently; others were changed in the past by having the original wood replaced by iron. The base of each cross is generally a hemisphere of stone bearing the initials B.A.P. (Baldassare Audibert Pax), with the date of the year the cross was raised (usually 1846).

Directions to two of the Audibert crosses:

The Federico Cross

This wooden cross stands on the national highway (SS 323) running towards Monte Amiata, near the Castel del Piano exit and at the crossroads with the road on the right to Colle Vergari. Note the lilies at the top of the cross and at the end of the horizontal beam. A face is depicted at the centre. On the base is the usual inscription: "B.A.P. 1846".

The Colle Vergari Cross

At the crossroads marked by the Federico Cross (see above), take the road to Colle Vergari. The road runs round the village, and the cross stands where it doubles back towards the houses. The original wood cross has been replaced by one in iron.

A complete list of the crosses – with map and photos – can be found on the Internet: www.progettoamiataimmagini.com/croci.html

---

* *"Baldassarre Audiberte*
Eats, drinks and carouses
Raising crosses at ever corner,
Whatever dickheads might think"

THE GARDEN OF DANIEL SPOERRI ⑩

Happiness at the end of the meadow

58038 Seggiano (GR)
Tel: 0564 950 805
E-mail: ilgiardino@ilsilene.it
www.danielspoerri.org/
Opening hours: from 1 April to 15 October, 14.30-19.30
Admission: 10 €. Students and children: 8 €
Children under 8 years old: free admission

Daniel Spoerri's garden is an extraordinary place. Created by the founder of the "New Realist" movement, the garden was opened in 1997 and provides a remarkable setting for around 100 works by more than 40 contemporary artists. Apart from the eyesore of overhead power cables, these sculptures, objects and installations are surrounded by unspoilt nature. When the gates open in the morning, the first visitors catch glimpses of rabbits, deer and squirrels scampering in the midst of these unusual works. Daniel Spoerri's aim was in fact to use the gentle Tuscan landscape to provide a natural backdrop for the art.

One such piece, by an artist who signs his work as "Not Vital", seems to show a man floating in the air against the façade of a building. What is most surprising, however, is how the area is "occupied" by figures that are apparently engaged in ordinary activities such as reading, knitting, or simply observing others.

It is a splendid experience. And a must for children, who will long remember their time spent in a garden totally given over to a sense of play.

THE REBUS OF THE CATHEDRAL

A signature in the form of a rebus

Cathedral of San Lorenzo
Piazza del Duomo
58100 Grosseto (GR)

On the façade of the cathedral of San Lorenzo in Grosseto there is a mysterious carving of a circle containing a rebus of initials. The solution in Latin reads *Soxus Rustichini Construxit Tempore Malavoltae Potestatis Roseti*, which can be translated as "Constructed by Sozzo Rustichini at the time of the Rule of Malavolti". It is simply the clever signature of the cathedral's builder.

NEARBY

Etruscan bowl in the Maremma Archaeological Museum

3, Piazza Baccarini - 58100 Grosseto (GR)
Tel: 0564 48 87 50
E-mail: maam@gol.grosseto.it
Opening hours: from 1 November to 28 February, Tuesday to Friday 9.00-13.00, Saturday and Sunday 9.30-13.00 and 16.30-19.00; 1 March to 30 April, Tuesday to Sunday 9.30-13.00 and 16.30-19.00; and 2 May to 31 October, Tuesday to Sunday 10.00-13.00 and 17.00-20.00. Admission: 5 €

In the first display case to your right as you enter the first room (Sala 1), there is one of the most remarkable objects in the museum's Etruscan collection: a black terracotta bowl (bucchero nero) inscribed with the Etruscan alphabet. Dating from the 6th century BC, it has belonged to the museum since 1875, although its origin is unclear. Did it come from

the ruins of Roselle, an Etruscan city located near the modern-day Grosseto, or from southern Etruria? It was not unusual for household objects to be decorated with the alphabet. We know that the Etruscans were a very literate people and therefore such objects were aides mémoire constantly available for consultation.

The mystery of the Etruscan language

While the Etruscan alphabet has been known for some time, the language itself still remains partially shrouded in mystery. Experts have translated about 20,000 inscriptions, most of them short and repetitive phrases that appear on funeral monuments.

This work was facilitated by the discovery in 1964 of the "Pyrgi Plates" (Pyrgi was one of the ports of the Etruscan city of Caere, the modern-day Cerveteri); two of these three gold plates bore the same text in Etruscan and Phoenician. But the entirety of known Etruscan texts has yet to be translated.

One of the main difficulties scholars face is that the language is an "isolated" one – that is, it is not part of any known linguistic group.

MONUMENT TO LEOPOLD II

(13)

Pray for Leopold II, Grand Duke of Tuscany

Road from Grosseto to Castiglione della Pescaia
Locality known as Badiola

C*anapone* ("Hemphead") is the friendly nickname that the people of the Maremma region – known for their lively disposition – bestowed on the last Grand Duke of Tuscany, Leopold II of Habsburg-Lorraine (1797-1870), because of his flaxen hair. This is a sign of the ties, at once affectionate and respectful, that bound the Grand Duke to Maremma and its inhabitants. Leopold II was fascinated by the wild nature of this region, and this is where he launched his grand plan of enlightened reforms and public works, including draining the malaria-infested swamp that surrounded Grosseto. The townspeople expressed their gratitude by erecting a grandiose statue in his honour, which still stands today in Piazza Dante at the heart of the town: he is shown helping to her feet a woman with a child in her arms.

On 27 April 1859, accompanied by his court, he left Florence, which together with the entire Tuscan territory would be annexed to the Kingdom of Italy a year later. Leopold II never returned. He went into self-imposed exile in Bohemia, but he always kept close to his heart the memory of his beloved Maremma, to which he devoted some moving passages in his last will and testament: *"... If Divine Providence should once again lead our family to our beloved land, our adored Tuscany, and entrust the government to my son Ferdinand, I commend Tuscany to your care: make sure that its fortune be thy glory, and the love you hold for it the reward for your care. Surround yourself with brothers who are real friends. I entrust you, my son, with your father's enterprises that you know so well. Maremma is the first patient, requiring assistance, fine and rich desolation. If you return to these lands, place on the road of Badiola, near Grosseto, a stone with a single cross, on which it shall be written: Pray for Leopold II, Grand Duke of Tuscany ..."* (16 July 1867).

This stone, on which a single cross was indeed engraved, was erected over a century later in memory of the Grand Duke. It lies on the road that links Grosseto with Castiglione della Pescaia at the precise spot known as Badiola, at the beginning of the tree-lined avenue that now leads to an exclusive resort – *Canapone* liked to stay in this villa (which was also a working farm) during his hunting parties.

GUILLOTINE IN THE ILDEBRANDO IMBERCIADORI LOCAL HISTORY MUSEUM

The last guillotine in Italy

Via Ugurgeri - 58030 Montepescali (GR)
Contact: Signor Castellani at 0564 32 91 40 (evenings only)
Opening hours: Wednesday to Sunday 15.00-18.30

Nicknamed the "Balcony of the Maremma", the village of Montepescali has a small local museum with numerous artefacts relating to local history: Etruscan and Roman pottery, old farming tools and implements, and archive documents providing details of the village's past. One of the main attractions is a clock mechanism that was stolen by Charles V's lansquenet mercenaries in 1555 and then rediscovered by chance in 1978 in the storerooms of the Museum of Geneva. But the

most unusual exhibit here is a reconstruction of a guillotine, which commemorates the village's connection with the last time such a machine was used in Grosseto: the victims were five bandits who, for a mere loaf of bread, had massacred the members of the Tacchia family in the Montepescali woods. Their execution took place on 18 November 1822.

The last execution by guillotine in Italy took place in Lucca on 29 July 1845, when five members of a band of brigands who had been terrorising the surrounding countryside were beheaded at the Porta San Donato. In 1847 the people of Lucca would actually hurl the blade of that guillotine into the sea at Viareggio, after setting fire to the wooden scaffold.

INSCRIPTIONS ON THE TORRE CANDELIERE

Names of traitors inscribed in stone

Torre del Candeliere. Piazza Matteotti
58024 Massa Marittima (GR)
Tel: 0566 90 22 89
E-mail: info@coopcollinemetallifere.it
The names carved on the outside of the tower can be seen from the street in Piazza Matteotti
To visit the inside of the tower:
Opening hours: from April to October, 10.00-13.00 and from 15.00-18.00; November to March, 11.00-13.00 and 14.30-16.30. Closed Monday.
Admission: 2.50 €

Raised to assert the autonomy of the free commune of Massa Marittima in 1228, the Torre del Candeliere was a powerful local symbol – so much so that when the Sienese captured the town in 1333 they had two-thirds of it demolished in order to humble the vanquished population. As a result, the tower, which once stood 74 metres tall, now only rises 24 metres. The Sienese occupierswould, however, build the elegant arch that links the tower to the ramparts, and reorganise the fortifications of the citadel. Their main concern in doing so was not attack from outside but rather the threat posed by local uprisings.

The inscriptions on the tower's stones are not immediately legible. One of them is in Latin and records the construction of the original tower in 1228, when Tedice Malabarba of Pisa was podestà. According to legend, the other inscription lists the traitors who helped the Sienese to take and sack the town in 1331. Certain historians support this claim, but a more likely theory is that the inscription gives the names of the assize court judge, Uberto Faselus, and the town camerario*(a certain Mellone) at the time the tower was originally built.

* *The camerario - or chamberlain - was responsible for the 'chamber' of a religious or political ruler. The term "chamber" here is used to cover all aspects of the figure's private life – primarily, the management of his financial interests. In the Catholic Church, the camerario apostolico is responsible for the running of the pope's personal household.*

THE SPRING OF ABUNDANCE AND THE TREE OF FECUNDITY

Dozens of male members in a 13th century fresco

Piazzale Mazzini
58024 Massa Marittima (GR)
Note: the fresco is undergoing restoration and, at the time of printing, was still not open to the public

The fresco within the porch containing the fountain in Piazza Mazzini will surprise even the most blasé hunters after the curious and bizarre. Painted in 1265 – the same year in which the fountain came into use – it depicts a tree bearing heavy fruit which, upon close inspection, turns out to be penises. The women standing beneath the laden branches are busy plucking the fruit and placing them in their baskets. Clearly allegorical in attention, this fresco is nevertheless very forthright in its realism – and demonstrates that religious subjects were not the only thing which attracted 13th century artists.

The fresco was only recently rediscovered after have lain for years "protected" by the thick layer of lime scale deposited by the water from the fountain – in fact , it had been effectively protected not only from the elements but also from the narrow-mindedness of those who would have been quick to censure such unorthodox work. Paradoxically, the removal of the lime scale damaged the fresco, so now the restoration has had to be reassessed by the Officio delle Pietri Dure in Florence. Hence the delay in the conclusion of work which, according to original estimates, should have been completed in 2005.

The name "Fountain of Abundance" does not allude to the copious flow of water but to the fact that the space above the arcade was given over to the storage of grain for use during periods of famine.

Arezzo and surroundings

FONDAZIONE ARCHIVIO
DIARISTICO NAZIONALE-ONLUS

Have your diary archived

Piazza Plinio Pellegrini, 1
52036 Pieve San Stefano (AR)
Tel: 0575 79 77 30 – 31
E-mail: adn@archividiari.it
www.archividiari.it
Opening hours: Monday to Friday 8.30-13.30 and 15.00-18.00, Saturdays
8.30-12.30

The original idea came from journalist and writer Saverio Tutino: in 1984 he founded this archive of Italian personal diaries, as well as the Pieve-Banca Toscana prize for the most interesting examples of this particular form of writing. Advertised without great fanfare in a few national newspapers, the competition was a success from the start, with more than a hundred diaries submitted in its first year. Today this memory bank, which the organisers prefer to refer to as a 'seedbed', has become an important and well-established resource: the Fondazione Archivio Diaristico Nazionale–onlus.

Was it the fact that the town centre here was razed to the ground by the Nazis in 1944 that made Pieve Santo Stefano particularly sensitive to the question of historical memory? Perhaps. But whatever the reason, it is true that every year the Pieve collection acquires about 150 personal diaries, autobiographies or collections of letters, with the Archives now holding more than 5,000 texts. A half-yearly publication, PrimaPersona, produced by the Foundation is on sale in branches of the Feltrinelli bookshop throughout Italy.

The premises serve not as a museum but as a library. And, unless stated to the contrary, the texts are available for consultation by scholars and the general public alike. Furthermore, more than a hundred university degree theses have been dedicated to this phenomenon (and their number increases each year); these too are available for consultation. From a material point of view, one of the most original works in the Archives comprises the personal memoirs of Clelia Marchi: after the death of her husband in 1984, she began to write the story of her life on her bed sheets.

NEARBY
The Campari Fountain ②

Piazza Caduti
52010 Chiusi della Verna (AR)
This fountain advertising Campari was produced in 1931 by the sculptor Giuseppe Gronchi. It was the first of a series of twelve identical fountains created throughout Italy. Amongst those still extant is another at Le Piastre, outside Pistoia.

ETRUSCAN OFFERINGS IN THE CASENTINO ARCHAEOLOGICAL MUSEUM

A thoughtful collection of expiatory gifts

Via Berni, 21 - Bibbiena (Province of Arezzo)
Open: Wed—Sun 10am—1pm and Fri—Sun 4pm—7pm. Closed on Friday afternoons October to April, with likely opening times reduced by half an hour.
Entry fee: Full entry 3€, reduced entry 1€
Tel: 0575-595-486 - Email: info@arcamuseocasentino.it
www.arcamuseocasentino.it

A new series of archaeological excavations began in 2003, as result of which, this museum in Bibbiena is now the home of the finest collection of man-made pieces uncovered at the Lake of the Idols. The craftsmanship of many of these items is superb, and even those that were mass produced are just as striking. They all seem to have been taken there with a common goal in mind. Complete human figures, arrowheads doubtless intended as offerings by warriors, figures of animals, and misshapen pieces of bronze used as a rudimentary currency have all been recovered from the lake. Mutilated statuettes of people and objects representing parts of the body found there suggest that the lake was visited by pilgrims and venerated as a place of healing, in spite of the fact that the waters have never had any curative powers.

We know from some of the discoveries that the first Romans were attracted to this lake, but they have not left any other records to enlighten us other than the large number of ex-votos found there. Most of the archaeological finds from the lake were sold in the 19th century; some now form part of private collections or are in museums in Paris or London, or in this museum at Bibbiena.

The Lake of Idols: a mysterious place of pilgrimage for the Etruscans

Until 1838, the Lake of Idols, a small circular stretch of water situated 1,380 metres above sea level, was known as the Lake of the Cherry Orchard. In ancient times it was a place of mystery visited by pilgrims of all social classes.

The incredible truth about this place surfaced (literally) in 1838 when a shepherdess chanced upon a splendidly crafted Etruscan statuette in the mud on the shore. It was not long before archaeological excavations were initiated, involving the total draining of the lake. The first series of digs in the 19th century alone yielded about 600 items of bronze or ceramic manufacture. And the fact that most of them originated outside this area, leads to the conclusion that this site was a focus for all Etruscans, irrespective of their place of origin.

After the 2003 dig, the lake was refilled in 2007. It is located in the immediate vicinity of the sources of the Arno on Monte Falterona and can only be reached on foot by following directions on signposts along the paths to Capo d'Arno or Laghetto degli Idoli.

THE GIANT STILL OF
THE CAMALDOLESE NUNS

A contraption of superhuman dimensions

Monastery of San Giovanni Evangelista
Piazza Jacopo Landino
Pratovecchio (Province of Arezzo)
Open: The still room can be visited on Saturday 8:30am—10:30am
Tel: 0575-583-767

n the oldest square in Pratovecchio, the Camaldolese nuns' Monastery of San Giovanni Evangelista conceals the town's great secret.

If you manage to persuade one of these elderly and very busy ladies to open the door for you, you will discover a room containing a kind of octagonal stone dome with rounded walls that stands about two metres high. The walls feature a number of openings made of terra cotta.

From as early as 1048, each Camaldolese nuns' monastery was attached to a hospital caring for poor people and pilgrims. Some also specialised in the art of pharmacy and essential chemistry.

The dome we are seeing here is a still of the *stufa secca* (dry stove) kind (see below). This example has its origins in the 12th or 13th century and is much larger and more ancient than any others that have been preserved or classified. It was a very innovative apparatus in so far as the number of openings in the walls ensured that several different preparations could be produced simultaneously. When in use, this instrument was located outside and heated by burning wood. There is good reason to believe that it stood taller then too, since it would have rested on bricks in order to raise it up to make it easier to collect the ashes.

How does a still work?

The *stufa secca*, a phrase frequently found in the names of medieval Italian towns, was a construction designed for distillation by means of an internal fire that heated its walls. These were fitted with openings (you can see the openings in the photo) into which glass bottles, closed with a "cap" that ended in a long neck, were inserted. The neck was in integral part of the cooling procedure and it was from there that the distilled liquid flowed. The *stufa secca* differed from the more primitive wet method, whereby the bottles were heated by steam from a water boiler that remained located inside the stove. The development of materials allowing the 'dry' distillation method resulted in a marked simplification of the work involved, prompting its use to become widespread. It was no longer necessary to constantly top up the water as from then on, all that was needed was to feed the fire and control its temperature.

THE WORLD FORGING CHAMPIONSHIP EXHIBITION

The art of converting iron into works of art

Autonomous Association of the Biennial Competition of the Blacksmiths' Art at Stia (Province of Arezzo)
Open: Visits on request in anticipation of the opening of the museum
Tel: 366-305-2558 - Email: info@biennaleartefabbrile.it
www.biennaleartefabbrile.it - www.comune.pratovecchiostia.ar.it

Stia is a hive of cultural activity. Since 1976 it has hosted the European biennial blacksmiths' art contest. This event has, since 1989, grown into a major iron forging championship.

The association that runs it consists solely of volunteers. It provides forges, anvils, iron and coal for the use of the participants. Blacksmiths come to Stia from all over the world in order to compete against one another. The aim of the competition is to forge a work according to a theme selected by the *Biennale*.

The centre of this old town is transformed into a veritable open-air smithy for the event. Raised platforms are erected at a safe distance for the public to watch some 200 blacksmiths perform. This ensures some protection from the intense heat the smiths require to achieve their results. Competitors have three hours to complete their tasks. The final piece must be forged from one solid piece of metal and no welding is allowed.

In the 40 years of the competition's history, an extensive collection of works has been produced, some of a very high standard. So restoration work has been undertaken on one of the floors of the town's old spinning mill to convert it into a museum. Ultimately the aim is that the association's collection will go on permanent display there. Each smith taking part provides one piece from the competition.

In anticipation of the opening of the museum, which is expected for the 2018 *Biennale*, works selected for future display can be seen in the warehouse where they are being temporarily housed. Others not included in the display, but no less beautiful, are offered for sale.

Other museums and places of interest in Stia

Apart from the famous Museum of the Art of Wool (see following double page), the little town of Stia has its Museum of Woods and Mountains, the "Carlo Beni" Ornithological Collection, and a fantastic skiing museum. Details of opening hours can be found at the following website:

www.comune.pratovecchiostia.ar.it/turismo/da-vedere/musei

CASENTINO FABRIC

Stylish bright coloured garments with a long history

Tessilnova, the Stia woollen mill
Via Giovanni Sartori, 2/4
Stia (Province of Arezzo)
Open: Shop opens Mon—Fri 9:30am—1pm and 3:30pm—7:30pm; Sat—Sun
9:30am—1pm and 3:30pm—8pm; Production stops on Saturdays and Sundays
Tel: 0575-582-685
Email: info@tessilnova.com
www.tessilnova.com

The famous Stia woollen mill industrialised its production in 1835 but had processed the region's wool for centuries before that. These changes were a tremendous achievement, not only in terms of industry but also in terms of the architecture of the new establishment. However, the greatest success resulting from these changes, as is often the case, came about by chance, or perhaps by mistake.

During the transition from natural to synthetic dyes, at a time when seconds counted in the effort to reach production on an industrial scale, there were skills gaps. A lack of staff experienced in reproducing a certain kind of red resulted in an error that produced a rather vivid orange. Against all expectations, this colour turned out to be enormously popular. More surprisingly, it was in particular demand in men's fashion of the time. The orange is indeed quite loud and sufficiently bright that it is used today to make clothes designed to combine high visibility with warmth.

This woollen cloth, with its traditional finish of minute curls, is known as Casentino. It is made using a special manufacturing technique. This process is applied to one side of the cloth to create a layer of tiny curls, and lends elegance to a rather thick woollen fabric — hence its appeal to country people in the old days.

The Tessilnova woollen mill is the last one still in use within this early industrial complex. Visitors can observe the various stages of the weaving process. While industrial looms now play an important part, traditional ways of production are followed as closely as possible in making these very distinctive clothes. New colours have also been added, but the charm of the orange coats and jackets remains.

The same building also houses the very well organised Museum of the Art of Wool, where all the stages in the manufacture of woollen garments are explained on an interactive walk involving sound, touch and smell. Use of the senses has always been key to the manufacture of cloth. The museum shows how wool manufacturing has evolved over the centuries, what techniques have remained the same, and which have been improved. What's more, it helps us understand how production in establishments like this one in Stia finally ended, and in this particular case how it became a museum. The museum's collection also includes many machines of great historical and technical value, some of them still set up in their original locations.

Website: www.museodellartedellalana.it

MUSEUM OF GUN POWDER AND SMUGGLING ⑦

A village that thrived on contraband

Via Verna
52010 Chitignano (AR)
Opening hours: From the last Saturday in June to the first Sunday in September,
15.00-19.00. At other times, visits possible by appointment
Tel: 0575 59 67 13 (8.00-14.00, except Sunday)
Free admission
To walk to the "Gunpowder Factory of Hell": take the SP60 towards Verna. After
a few bends in the road, the route is marked by a post bearing the number one,
indicating the beginning of the footpath; there is not much car parking space.
Now follow the footpath to the pillo [crushing plant]

Set up in 2001, the Museum of Gunpowder and Smuggling in Chitignano is a fine way of paying homage to the village's disreputable past as a centre of contraband. In 1789 the Tuscan government forbade the sale of tobacco and introduced limits on how much could be grown for personal consumption. Threatened with the loss of one of their major sources of income, the inhabitants of Chitignano decided to ignore the ban and become smugglers, buying tobacco in Umbria, processing it in Chitignano, and then transporting it northwards.

Later, in 1830, the Grand Duchy of Tuscany introduced a total ban on the growing of tobacco. At this point, Chitignano looked for another source of income. There were already two licensed gunpowder factories in the area, so the inhabitants set to producing and distributing contraband gunpowder. The smugglers acquired the sulphur and saltpetre secretly and then produced charcoal using the wood of the area's abundant walnut trees.

The museum gives you a vivid picture of the activities of the smugglers. Furthermore, a ten-minute walk along a path marked by numbered posts brings you to the "Gunpowder Factory of Hell", which contains a fully

functional crushing plant built of wood. Driven by a waterwheel powered by a small stream flowing through this magnificent - and secluded - area of woodland, the plant was used to mix the three basic ingredients of gunpowder...

NEARBY
Model in the Museum of the Battle of Anghiari ⑧

1-2, Piazza Mameli - 52031 Anghiari (AR)
Tel: 0575 78 70 23
Opening hours: April to October, daily 9.00-19.00; November to March, Friday,
Saturday and Sunday 9.00-13.00 and 15.00-19.00. Admission: 3.50 €

A fine model recreates the Battle of Anghiari, which was of great importance in the history of Tuscany: fought on 29 June 1440, this clash between Florentine forces (commanded by Niccolò Piccinino) and a Milanese army resulted in a victory which saved Tuscany from becoming a dominion of the Duke of Milan. Machiavelli later gave this ironic account of the battle: "And if this combat which was so long that it lasted from twenty to twenty-four hours, not a single man died from wounds caused by weapons or other valorous feats of arms, but only as a result of falling from his horse and being trodden under hoof."

Baldaccio's ghost still haunts the Castello di Sorci

Built during the 13th century, the Castello di Sorci [Castle of Mice] was for fifty years home to the family of Baldaccio d'Anghiari, a "soldier of fortune" (capitano di ventura) born around 1400. Baldaccio's career began when he recruited a band of mercenaries to pillage the surrounding area. He was twice sentenced to the gallows, but then "saved" by the Florentines whom he served on various occasions.

Unfortunately for Baldaccio, he would denounce Bartolomeo Orlandini for cowardice in abandoning the castle of Marradi to the troops of another capitano di ventura (Niccolò Piccinino, 1386-1444; so-called because he was short of stature: piccinin).

When Orlandini became Gonfaloniere di Giustizia in Florence, he took revenge: on 6 September 1441, he summoned Baldaccio to Palazzo Vecchio, accused him of treason, had him stabbed several times and then hurled his body out of the window.

Baldacci survived – only to be beheaded; afterwards his body was put on public display. Since that treacherous death, it would seem that Baldaccio's ghost has haunted his family castle, which can be visited by applying at the restaurant or (for group visits) by prior phone booking. Don't forget to try the wonderful home-made pasta, washed down with a good bottle of vino del fantasma.

"Castello di Sorci" Hotel. 52031 Anghiari (AR). Tel: 0575 78 90 66. E-mail: info@castellodisorci.it. www.castellodisorci.it
Closed Mondays. Visits to the castle : 1 €. Free for children. Vino del fantasma: 4 € per 3/4 litre. Directions: from Anghiari take the road to Arezzo, the castle stands about 3 km down the road.

CLOCK TOWER

The largest "Roman" clock face in Italy

Castello di San Niccolò
52018 Castel San Niccolò (AR)
To find out more: www.nicolaseverino.it

The clock at the castle of San Niccolò is curious in that it has a "Roman" clock face – that is, one which marks out of the hours of the day from I to VI, rather than I to XII (see below). Whilst the castle itself dates back to the 13th century, the clock dates from 1806-1807 and its mechanism was replaced in 1863. It is of such massive size because it was intended to be visible to the peasants working in the surrounding fields.

The measurement of time

The division of a day into hours probably began with the Chaldeans. We know that the Babylonians divided the day into 12 kaspars and the Chinese into 12 toki. The Greeks and the Romans would divide the day into two equal periods of twelve hours each. Given that the period of daylight varied according to the season, the length of these day or night hours could vary, with an hour of winter daytime being much shorter than an hour of winter night time.

The need for a more precise measurement of time was felt by certain rigorously disciplined monastic orders, particularly the Benedictines, who used sundials to fix the hours of prayers (matins, vespers, etc) with precision.

Mechanical clocks would make their first appearance in Europe at the end of the 13th century. This entailed a veritable revolution: now hours had a fixed length, and by the end of the 14th century, most cities had abandoned sundials and gnomons for mechanical clocks installed in church towers.

Beginning at sunset, the day was divided into 24 hours, with the clock face thus being marked from I to XXIV. However, it was soon realised that having to count up to 24 strokes of the clock in order to tell the time could lead to error.

In the 15th century a simplified system was adopted, with clocks striking a maximum of 6 times rather than 24. This simplification in counting the strokes of the hour was soon reflected in clock faces, which were now marked I to VI (like the one here at San Niccolò).

During the period of Napoleonic rule, this "Roman" clock face was replaced with the "French-style" clock face marked I to XII, with the day beginning not at sunset but at midnight.

KNOTTED COLUMNS IN THE CHURCH OF GROPINA

The secret message of Gropina

Church of Saint-Pierre (Pieve di San Pietro), Gropina
52024 Loro Ciuffenno (AR)
Opening hours: In winter 8.00-12.00 and 15.00-17.00, summer, 8.00-12.00 and from 17.00-19.00
Directions: Take the Valdarno exit off the A1 motorway. Follow the SP1 to Loro Ciuffena. After driving through the town, continue on the same road (also called Via dei Sette Ponti) towards Arezzo. After 1.3 km, take the narrow unsurfaced road to the village of Gropina

G ropina church, built in the 12th century over 4th- and 8th-century structures, possesses an interior of great sobriety: this shows off the imposing pulpit, covered with occult symbols that were probably left by a medieval guild of master builders.

The builders were probably hired by the Countess Matilde de Canossa (or Matilda of Tuscany) (1046-1115), whose head is carved above the main entrance to the church. She was an ardent supporter of the papacy, a feminist and protector of women in need, cultured, a Catholic and certainly sympathetic to the hermetic knowledge of the time.

Thus on the pulpit (the place for the sermon, eloquence and the creative word) can be seen a sculpture of the goddess Melusine, Lady of the Waters of Creation. Above there is another mythical figure, flanked by two serpents that meet level with the head of Melusine, seeming to want to swallow her. This represents the *Uroborus* (or *Ouroboros*), the serpent biting its tail, a symbol of eternity, Wisdom and the Pantocrator, i.e. of God the Creator of Heaven and Earth.

Interestingly, these characters from the pantheon of ancient gods are harmoniously transposed here among Christian symbols, a reminder that Christianity, far from starting from scratch, gradually assimilated pre-Christian symbols and traditions. Thus on the front of the pulpit you find the evangelists represented by animals: the eagle for St. John, the angel for St. Matthew, the lion for St. Mark. The bull for St. Luke is missing, as he is represented by the pulpit itself, which is rather surprisingly supported by two columns attached by what looks like a knot. Although Gropina's priest, Don Valente Moretti, says: "*One of the columns represents the Father, the other the Son and the knot that unites them, the Holy Spirit. The whole forming the Holy Trinity*", others think that the symbolism could also be the two natures of the Son of God, human and divine, gathered together in one person by the knot.

In pre-Christian tradition (note another knot on a column outside the apse, which Father Moretti sees only as a decorative element), the knot also recalls the body of a serpent, indicating the presence of the telluric energy of the Earth, where fertility is represented by the bull, as well as the Word (symbolised by the sermon at the pulpit) that became flesh, as the Bible says.

Continued on following double-page spread.

The capitals of the pillars and columns in the church also recall the symbols of ancient tradition and the Christian religion.

Entering by the main door you'll see, starting from the first pillar on the right, a sow and her four piglets as well as a male and female wolf devouring a lamb. The sow is a reminder of abundance and the piglets recall the four seasons, because once they are killed their meat will supply food for the whole year.

The she-wolf with open jaws and the male wolf devouring the lamb signify the opposite of abundance: barren seasons heralding famine and misery in peasant society. From a theological perspective, the sow represents the secular state, and the she-wolf (*lupa*) the occult state (like the Moon – *lupe* – that hides from the Sun) of what is revealed.

The first column on the right also features a knight (Faith) on horseback (Tradition), armed with shield and spear (Protection and the Ideal) and fighting two demons. The spear pierces both the head of one (Heresy) and the belly of the other (Lust). On a higher plane, the knight will represent the Spirit (Sun), the Soul (Moon) and the Body (Earth): and above all the knight is also seeking control of the soul and body (the two demons) to move forward in his spiritual initiation (the Sun).

In the Middle Ages, hunting wild boar brought back memories of the medieval noble art of hunting, which was always about acquiring the Wisdom of the World through death or by overcoming worldliness and the profane condition, represented by the animal.

On the first column from the left, there is also the surprising figure of a masked demon surrounded by plant motifs, suggesting the traditional "green man", an allegory of the Spirit of Nature that provides men with the abundance of produce necessary for their survival. This legacy of the agrarian tradition of primitive peoples was symbolically transformed by Christianity into the figure of the Holy Spirit, purveyor of Life and Evolution, celebrated at Pentecost. This is the Jewish heritage of the Feast of Firstfruits, in accordance with the interpretation of the "green man" taken as a symbol of rebirth, i.e. representing the cycle of growth each spring, when the new astrological year begins (21 March in the northern hemisphere), called the "northern spring". This event was celebrated by ancient agrarian peoples who depicted him as a diabolical or supernatural figure covered with leaves and fruit.

The panel representing the Gospel according to St. Matthew bears a Latin inscription stating that it was the priest Bernard, in the year 825, who had the pulpit built, even though it has subsequently undergone many modifications.

TROMPE-L'ŒIL CUPOLA IN THE CHURCH OF LA BADIA

A cupola that is an illusion

Piazza della Badia
52100 Arezzo (AR)

Built by Benedictine monks in the 13th century, the church of Sante Flora e Lucilla was altered extensively by Giorgio Vasari in 1565. It has an astonishing *trompe-l'œil cupola* created by Andrea Pozzo in 1702; recent restoration has made the optical illusion even more stunning in effect.

Andrea Pozzo created two other trompe-l'oeil cupolas: one in the university church of Vienna, the other in the church of San Ignazio in Rome (see *Secret Rome*, by the same publisher).

NEARBY ⑫
A crooked column

Some precious treasures are kept in the Romanesque room of Santa Maria, but the church has two further features of interest. With its Cycle of the Seasons, the 12th-century façade is one of very few examples of medieval sculpture to have actually kept their original colours. In addition, one of the columns in the apse on the Piazza Grande appears to be kneeling. It has been suggested that this kneeling attitude might be the signature of the architect, but there is no evidence to support this theory.

THE ASTRONOMICAL CLOCK OF THE LAY FRATERNITY ⑬

The last manually wound astronomical clock in the world

Piazza Grande - 52100 Arezzo (AR)
Open: Daily 10:30am—6pm
Entry fee: Adults 4€ with a guide, 3€ without. Ticket includes a visit to the picture gallery (see box below)
Tel: 057-524-694 - Email: info@museodifraternita.it - www.museodifraternita.it

The Palazzo of the Lay Fraternity, a fine building in its own right, was further embellished in 1552 by the addition of a wonderful astronomical clock, built by the master clockmaker Felice da Fossato and no doubt the last hand wound one in the world. Legend has it that his sponsors blinded or even murdered him after completing the work to prevent him from reproducing one like it elsewhere. Whether or not that is true, the fact remains that this is a very beautiful clock. What we see is entirely original, apart from one of the gears, which was replaced in the 19th century, and the pendulum, which was added in 1686, not long after pendulums were invented.

The clock's mechanism uses a counterweight system with ropes equivalent in length to the height of two floors. The weights are attached to these ropes and this moves the clock's single hand to indicate the time in hours and half hours. It also activates the cables to the bells that inform the public of the time. Finally, it drives hands that depict the sun and the moon, which revolve around the Earth, fixed in the centre following the Ptolemaic system. The moon, a black and gold sphere, rotates on its own axis to indicate to the country folk times of reaping and sowing.

The cell housing the mechanism includes a meridian to be referred to daily at noon to assist with regulating the precise time. But the meridian's original function became redundant as soon as the pendulum was fitted to the clock, because the latter effectively reduced slow running to a minimum, unlike before when slow running accumulated, making regular adjustment necessary.

The clock has to be wound up every day or, to be more precise, every 26-27 hours — giving a few hours leeway to the person tasked with winding it up. A purpose-built handle is used to rewind the ropes bearing the weights. This daily procedure resets the mechanism that for about 500 years has kept the clock running. Nowadays the clock is wound up at exactly 5pm to coincide with the guided visit that begins at 4:30pm.

Founded in 1262, the Lay Fraternity has always been renowned for providing help in the pursuit of study and culture. It has provided study bursaries continuously since the 16th century and it was instrumental in creating the first public library in the town. A visit to the clock includes entry to the picture gallery, which houses some works of significance, including portraits of famous men who have lent encouragement to the fraternity over the years. There is also a very fine picture showing a view of the Piazza Grande at the time of the Rinascimento.

THE PORTA CRUCIFERA SARACEN ⑭ JOUST MUSEUM

Golden lances and the colourful trappings of the Saracen Joust

Palazzo Alberti
Via San Nicolò della Minerva,1 - 52100 Arezzo (AR)
Visits are free and by appointment only - Tel: 380-502-7178

During Arezzo's Saracen Joust, four separate *quartieri* (areas of the city) come face to face in a tournament in the Piazza Grande. As well as its own headquarters, club and meeting room, each competing *quartiere* has its own museum. The most outstanding museum belongs to the *quartiere* of Porta Crucifera, chiefly because over the centuries it has carried off more victories than any of the others — 37 in total. It is every

bit as proud of its headquarters, which is also situated here in this fine historic palace.

Some of the finest objects displayed in the museum are its golden lances, actually made of wood and painted gold. These lances are the coveted trophies won in the tournament. Each lance is unique, hand crafted in the same workshop, and each is dedicated to a different theme depending on the occasion. The *quartiere* also boasts of a prize list that includes a whole dynasty of winning jousters — a grandfather, father and son all members of the Vannozzi family! Also forming part of the museum's treasures is a colourful collection of the costumes, saddles, crossbows and other accessories used in the historical procession as it crosses the city on its way to the joust. This parade is as important an element of the day as the tournament itself, and just as spectacular.

The Saracen Joust: a tradition dating back to the Crusades

The joust is both an historical and cultural event kept alive with great enthusiasm in Arezzo. It takes place twice a year: the third Saturday in June and the first Sunday in September. The four *quartieri* of the city (Porta Crucifera, Porta Sant'Andrea, Porta del Foro and Porta Santo Spirito) compete with each other, jousting on horseback. Each knight charges with his wooden lance (weighing about 6 kilos!) with the aim of striking a shield mounted on a dummy called the *buratto*. On impact with the lance, the *buratto* pivots round swinging three iron balls covered with leather (the *mazzafrusto*) towards the knight who must avoid being struck by them. This practice is ancient and probably dates back as far as the Crusades in the 13th century. Tradition has it that the enemy in the tournament is a Saracen and that the knight is throwing down a challenge to him. The Saracen's shield is in fact a target, and the knight needs to aim for the highest scoring zones. There are very precise rules governing the joust: if a knight drops his lance on impact with the *buratto* he loses all his points; but if he breaks his lance on impact, he doubles them. Here is an interesting rule: if the lance strikes the Saracen anywhere else but on his shield, the knight is disqualified on the basis that following the rules of chivalry, honour is a fundamental part of single combat even if you despise your enemy. The Piazza Grande is itself a hive of activity throughout the year. And the event could not take place without the willing participation of the voluntary association members on whom the *quartieri* so heavily rely. Their work includes regularly organising dinners and other activities, such as a drumming school, not to mention the management of its own clubs and museums (see opposite page).

The joust is preceded by a colourful procession in period costume, which, after the blessing at the cathedral, marches across town to reach the Piazza Grande shortly before the tournament begins. The costume characters in the procession *(quartieristi)* are made up of people who live in of each of the four areas. Once on the square, the participants in the procession lay down their weapons in specially reserved spaces and line up on both sides of the lists, the track across the Piazza where the jousters will charge.

The day includes a performance by the standard-bearers of Arezzo, who dazzle with their amazing flag-waving skills. On a day like this, everybody has a part to play and the costumed supporters of the *quartieri* are very much part of what makes the day as they support their team from the side of the lists and march through the town in procession.

To attend the Saracen Joust, contact the town council on the above website or else write to the following email address: jacopo@jacopodellatorre.com.

THE WILD WEST COLLECTION

An incredible collection of historic firearms

Piazza Grande, 6
52100 Arezzo (AR)
Open: First Sunday of each month, when the antiques market is open. Ask there where you can find the "Wild West" (otherwise known as Sandro Brizzolari) and if the owner is around, he will be happy to open up for you.

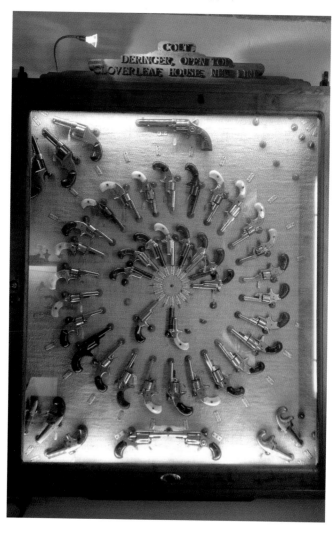

Arezzo is popular amongst antique dealers and collectors. Starting in 1971, one resident of the town, whose passion for westerns has gripped him since childhood, has built up an excellent collection of guns, pistols and other firearms. It consists of 800 firearms used during the conquest of the West in the United States. Everything in the collection is totally genuine down to the last detail. Sandro Brizzolari acquired these weapons over the years during his travels around the world, especially in America. Everything is in perfect condition and certified genuine by historic documentation, with the exception of one Colt whose original documentation was destroyed in 1864.

Brizzolari is hesitant to reveal which firearm is the oldest, the most rare or the most valuable, because in his eyes they are all of equal importance. Acquiring each of them has presented some kind of challenge, whether it involved correct application of the rules, or dealing with a lack of understanding, a lack of interest or even sheer narrow-mindedness.

Visitors can see beautifully decorated pistols, guns powerful enough to stop a locomotive, or so tiny that they can be slipped into a garter or a pocket; there are handguns with an internal hammer (affectionately known as "lemon squeezers") and pistols that can be concealed in the palm of the hand; special devices for making cartridges, and a whole range of guns and other apparatus created to demonstrate to vendors of the day how a new product functioned. There are other related items, including original ammunition and spare grips — if you're tired of the wooden one why not swap if for ivory? There is even a fine library specialising in works on firearms of that time; the documentation and gun collection is unique and must be the most extensive in Europe, probably even the world.

MUSEUM OF THE GORI & ZUCCHI COMPANY (Uno A Erre) ⑯

Saddam Hussein's silver sword

550, Via Fiorentina,
52100 Arezzo (AR)
Visits – either free or guided tours – by appointment only
Tel: 0575 92 54 03.
E-mail: museo.info@unoaerre.it

One of the world's leading creators of jewellery and costume jewellery, Uno A Erre has a museum within its premises in Arezzo. Along with a wide range of the pieces which the company has manufactured since its foundation in 1926, there are also tools and instruments and various original designs.

One of the showcases contains the steel jewellery that was created in response to the Oro alla Patria [Gold for the Fatherland] campaign (see below).

The most unusual piece in the museum, however, is a silver sword that was presented to the dictator Saddam Hussein in 1986. This was the model for the 150 gold swords encrusted with precious stones that Saddam was going to present as gifts to the various sheiks who had supported him in the war against Iran. In fact, 100 of these swords were delivered, but the wars in which Iraq was involved from 1990 onwards led to production being suspended.

Photograph courtesy of the Uno A Erre company

Gold for the fatherland

In response to the Fascist invasion of Ethiopia, the League of Nations (the first attempt at a United Nations) imposed economic sanctions on Italy. The Italian government's response was to collect as much gold as possible from individual citizens, given that the currency of the day was still bound to the gold standard. 18 December thus became "Confidence Day", with married couples offering their gold wedding rings in exchange for rings of steel.

After 1940, the collection was extended to cover steel itself, required in armaments factories. Mussolini was not the first to come up with this idea: the governments of both France and Great Britain had launched similar campaigns during the First World War.

PALAZZO MANCINI

Showing the Grim Reaper the door...

Via Dardano, 15
52044 Cortona (AR)

To the left of the main doorway of Palazzo Mancini is a remarkable example of a "Dead Man's Gate". A frequent feature in medieval buildings, these doorways had one function: to give egress to coffins. The door was then shut immediately so that the dead had no chance of re-entering the building. The custom seems to have come from the Etruscans, who believed that death itself exited with the dead man and that it could only come back via the same doorway. The subject is rather delicate, but it would seem that some of these doorways are still in use in Italy.

There is a second "Dead Man's Gate" in Cortona, at number 25 Via Roma; however, this one has been bricked in.

NEARBY
Saint Gilibert's Well

Saint Gilibert is said to have transformed the water from this well into wine.
The local road to Manzano (recently renamed Viale Vannucio Faralli). Monsigliolo - 52044 Cortona (AR)

The well is to the right of the local Manzano road which links Cortona with Foiano di Chiana. Just after the village of Monsigliolo there is a plaque which records a popular tradition that, in the year 515, St. Gilibert passed through here on a pilgrimage (probably heading for Rome) and stopped at this well, which is now named after him. To thank the peasant farmer for his hospitality, he changed the water drawn from the well into wine.

PONTE BURIANO

Mona Lisa's bridge?

52100 Arezzo (AR)

Built in 1277, the present Ponte Buriano would seem to stand on the site of a bridge built by the Etruscans to link the two cities of Arezzo and Fiesole. The span of that bridge rested on massive tree trunks, and the structure would later be incorporated by the Romans into their Via Cassia, which ran from Rome to Florence by way of Arezzo. The present bridge has survived thanks to the extraordinary efficiency of the bomb squads working with the Allied forces in 1944, who managed to defuse explosive charges set by the Germans as they retreated.

We know that in 1502 Leonardo da Vinci was commissioned by Cesare Borgia to draw up a map of this part of Tuscany. These maps now known as the "Windsor Maps" because they form part of the Royal Collection at Windsor Castle – show the Ponte Buriano. This fact has led some to conclude, perhaps rather hastily, that the bridge in question is the same as that which appears in the background to the right of the Mona Lisa. The supporters of this theory point out that the landscape on the left of the sitter has two other features typical of the area around Arezzo: meandering waterways entering a gorge, and marlaceous terrain. Others have argued that Leonardo simply created an imaginary landscape made up of elements taken from various places. It should be noted, however, that no other bridge has been put forward as a possible source for that which appears in the great painting.

NEARBY

Ivan Bruschi's Home Museum

14, Corso Italia - 52100 Arezzo (AR)
Tel: 0575 35 41 26 - E-mail: info@fondazionebruschi.it
www.fondazionebruschi.it
Opening hours: Tuesday to Sunday 10.00-13.00 and 17.00-19.00
(winter: 14.00-18.00)
Admission: 3 €, reduced: 2 €

A visit to this home-museum gives you an insight into the world of a 20th century visionary. An antiquarian and collector, Ivan Bruschi had a love of all things beautiful, and his magnificent home bears witness to a life dedicated to discovering the rare and notable artefacts of the past. What makes the place so unusual are the objects and furnishings that give us a very personal idea of this searcher after the curious and the intriguing. For example, the collection of coins (more than 4,000 extremely rare pieces) is housed in a piece of 18th century furniture. Composed of separate compartments which themselves contain a number of individual drawers, this piece of furniture is itself a little masterpiece of cabinet-making. Ivan Bruschi was also the original force behind the monthly Antiques Fair held in Arezzo, launching the very first one in 1968. The Fair is now held on the last Saturday/first Sunday of the month, from 8am to 8pm.

CHIANTI SCULPTURE PARK

A truly unique modern art park

S.P.9, near La Fornace, 48/49
Pievasciata (Province of Siena)
Open: Daily 10am until dusk
Entry fee: 10€
Tel: 0577-357-151
www.chiantisculpturepark.it

The Chianti Sculpture Park was created in the Sienese part of the Chianti as a permanent exhibition of installations and works of contemporary sculpture. It is located in the hamlet of Pievasciata, about 10 kilometres north of Siena.

The park comprises an area of 13 hectares of natural woods of holm oaks and sweet chestnut trees where wild boar were once bred. It came into being on the initiative of Piero and Rosalba Giadrossi, both contemporary art enthusiasts. After five years of preparatory work, the Sculpture Park, or Parco Sculture, was opened in 2004. It stretches along a one kilometre route, giving visitors the opportunity to enjoy impressive works by 27 highly reputable artists hailing from five continents. The idea for each work is suggested by the artist after visiting the woods in person and identifying his or her chosen spot for the exhibit to be installed, in such a way that the work totally complements its natural surroundings without having any detrimental effect whatsoever.

There are three principles on which the park was founded and continues to evolve: the integration of art with nature, multiculturalism of the artists, and the range of materials used (whether bronze or iron, granite or marble, glass or neon, or whatever else). As the seasons change so the settings of the exhibits become more evocative, thus lending the park an even greater uniqueness.

Exhibits found at the park include a work by Greece's Costas Varotsos, which is suggestive of a whirlwind emerging from the rocks and reaching for the sky. The installation by Turkey's Kemal Tufan is a stately ship's keel in volcanic lava. And English artist William Furlong's walk of steel (with acoustic effects activated by the passage of visitors) recreates the atmosphere typical of the streets of Siena.

Some of the sculptures are designed to interact with the public, such as the 80-metre wander through English artist Jeff Saward's maze, or the two platforms of travertine and marble separated by a small dip, which invite visitors to sit down and have an upright conversation with nature.

The park is also equipped with an amphitheatre. Its stage is backed with white Carrara marble extracted from the Michelangelo quarries and black granite from Zimbabwe, while the stage itself and terraced seats are built from slabs of volcanic lava.

A few metres from the park, Pievasciata's ancient kiln, a fine example of industrial technology, now hosts an art gallery that has brought together a large collection of national and international works under one roof.

MILK TAP AT THE OLD HOSPITAL ㉒ OF THE FRATERNITÀ DI SANTA MARIA

An automatic milk dispenser, dating from the 17th century

Piazza XX Settembre
53043 Chiusi (SI)

Against the wall inside the portico of the old hospital is the case which used to contain the "wheel" by means of which parents could leave their abandoned infants. The system worked on the same principle as that at the Ospedale degli Innocenti in Florence (see page 131).

Above this is a sort of twin-tube public dispenser in the form of two breasts. These would, upon demand, supply the children of poor families with milk. Two Latin inscriptions explain the purpose of this unusual facility, installed in 1620 thanks to a certain Borghese Samuelli. One reads Ad tutoria expositorum cunabula – 1620 and might be translated "For a safer sradle for foundlings". The second reads Charitatis ubera et meliora vino: the milk of charity is better than wine !

NEARBY

Two rival towers with astonishing names ㉓

At the Chiusi turn-off, the Villastrada road is flanked by two towers with astonishing names. One is Torre Beccati Questo [Take This Tower] and the other Torre Beccati Quello [Take That Tower]. In very different styles and some few hundred metres apart, one stands in Umbria and the other in Tuscany. They are clearly yet another expression of the ancient rivalry between the two regions.

THE COLUMN WITH A SERPENT

Lest you forget to observe the commandments and lose faith in God

Chiusi Cathedral - Piazza Duomo, 1 - 53043 Chiusi (SI)
Open: Daily from early morning until late evening

Inside Chiusi Cathedral, to the left of the main entrance, you will notice at the top of a granite column dating back to the days of ancient Rome, a bronze sculpture of a serpent.

The significance and presence of this serpent inside the church seems puzzling at first, especially since in the pagan world the serpent was believed to be an animal with prophetic powers, or else a symbol of the regenerative power of nature. The explanation is revealed in the Book of Numbers (21), in the part describing the road that led the Jews to the Red Sea, and in particular when the people exhausted by the long walk turn on Moses:

"Wherefore have ye brought us up out of Egypt to die in the wilderness? for there is no bread, neither is there any water; and our soul loatheth this light bread. And the Lord sent fiery serpents among the people, and they bit the people; and much people of Israel died. Therefore the people came to Moses, and said, We have sinned, for we have spoken against the Lord, and against thee; pray unto the Lord, that he take away the serpents from us. And Moses prayed for the people. And the Lord said unto Moses, Make thee a fiery serpent, and set it upon a pole: and it shall come to pass, that every one that is bitten, when he looketh upon it, shall live. And Moses made a serpent of brass, and put it upon a pole, and it came to pass, that if a serpent had bitten any man, when he beheld the serpent of brass, he lived."

According to Christian interpretation, the bronze serpent had no power but simply served to remind people to observe the commandments and have faith in God our healer and saviour. In other words, it is an allegorical representation of the cross on which the Son of God was crucified. "And as Moses lifted up the serpent in the wilderness, even so must the Son of man be lifted up: That whosoever believeth in him should not perish, but have eternal life." (Gospel according to St. John 3:14)

You will in fact see another granite pillar with an actual bronze cross opposite the central entrance to the Cathedral.

Ancient belief has it that "on the day of the Last Judgement, the bronze serpent will shed its rings to become flesh; after hissing with its tongue three times, it will crawl back into the Valley of Josaphat where the hands of Moses will work on it."

Another example of a column with a serpent at its top can be seen in the Basilica of Sant'Ambrogio in Milan — see *Secret Milan* from the same publisher.

ALPHABETICAL INDEX

ALPHABETICAL INDEX

ACKNOWLEDGEMENTS BY JACOPO MAURO:

My parents

Piero Taddei, Giulio Moscaritolo, Franz della Mea, Virgilio Contrucci, Massimo Adriano Betti, Carlo Querci, Giovanna Zurlo, Ilaria Bacherini, Paolo Grassi, Mario Ricci, Prof. Cesare Mancini, Paolo Orsucci, Maria Gemma Bendoni, Fabio Cannoni e la Contrada del Leocorno, Francesco Trenti, don Ugo Pineschi, Laura Davitti, Prof. Gerardo Gelardi, Marco Bartolini, Franco Galligani, Giuliano Bini, Orlando Papei, Alessandro Brizzolari, Marta Beneforti, Francesca Camilli, Anna Bonsignori, Alessandro Pommella, Alessio Pellegrini, Francesca Giunti, Gianluca Iori, Daniela Fattori, Chiara Marcheschi, Marcello Bianchi, L'Associazione Buddhista della Comunità Cinese in Italia.

ACKNOWLEDGEMENTS BY CARLO CASELLI:

Claudia Pussini Soso for her culture

Suzanne Boudeau for the reading

Sabrina Bertelli, Claudia Bolognesi, Debora Brocchini, Prof. Filippo Camerota, Silvano Carletti, Mauro Civai, Gessica Daveri, Angela De Luca, Marco Del Francia, Gloria Fiorini, Dominique Fuchs, Caroline Gallois, Giovanni Gaspari, Giuseppe Gavazzi, Dtt.ssa Sabina Ghilli, Vittorio Giorgini, Giovanni Guarneri, Grazia Lippi, Linda Lorenzetti, Giuseppe Marucchi, Anibale Parisi, Roberta Pirraccioli, Dtt.ssa Patrizia Salvadori, Luigi Scabia, Licinia Scardigli, Fabio Soso, Alberto Suci, Marcello Tiezzi, Vanni Desideri, Alberghi JK Place (Firenze), Palazzo Niccolini (Firenze),Villa Fontelunga, Castello di Montalto.

PHOTOGRAPHY CREDITS:

All photos by Carlo Caselli, with the exception of:
Accademia Internazionale d'Organo Giuseppe Gherardeschi: DR
Affreschi Casa Datini: Jacopo Mauro - Alambicco gigante: Jacopo Mauro - Arborario Montalcino: Jacopo Mauro - Bagni termali abbandonati: Jacopo Mauro - Biblioteca e sala concerto Chigiana: Giulio Moscaritolo - Bicchrena: Giulio Moscaritolo - Bosco romantico-esoterico: Jacopo Mauro - Campionato forgiatura: Jacopo Mauro - Cantine Contucci: DR - Castello Verrucosa: Antonello Trivelli per conto del Comune di Fivizzano - Castiglione del Terrier: Walter Bilotta - Cave di Terzo: Jacopo Mauro - Collezione privata bottiglie: Giulio Moscaritolo - Cimitero ebraico Pisa: Comunità Ebraica di Pisa - Una colonna storta: Jacopo Mauro - Fibonacci San Nicola Pisa: Jacopo Mauro - Fonti di Follonica: Giulio Moscaritolo - Fortezza Radicofani: Jacopo Mauro - Ghiacciaia Madonnina: Jacopo Mauro - Giostra del Saracino: Francesco Manetti - La grotta del Romito: Roberto di Fernando - Lance d'oro: Jacopo Mauro - Monastero e Conservatorio di San Niccolò: DR - Monumento-omaggio al Granduca di Toscana, Leopoldo II d'Asburgo-Lorena: Roberto di Fernando - Museo Archeologico Casentino: DR - Museo archeologico e d'arte della Maremma : DR - Museo Antartide: Giulio Moscaritolo - Museo Contrada Liocorno: Giulio Moscaritolo - Museo della Collegiata di Sant'Andrea : DR - Museo Deportazione e Resistenza: DR - Museo e refuge SMI: Jacopo Mauro - Orificio Clementi: Jacopo Mauro - Orologio astronomico Arezzo: Jacopo Mauro - Panno Casentino: Jacopo Mauro - Passeggiata Liberty a Lucca: Roberto di Fernando - Ponte Sospeso ferriere: Jacopo Mauro - Qual è l'origine del gallo nero del chianti?: Roberto di Fernando - I segreti di Piazza del Campo: Giulio Moscaritolo e Jacopo Mauro - Sistema dei musei di Massa Marittima: DR - Tempio Buddista San Bao: Jacopo Mauro - Torre del Lago: Jacopo Mauro - Uno A Ere : DR - Wild West: Alessandro Brizzolati, Jacopo Mauro

Maps: Cyrille Suss - **Layout Design:** Coralie Cintrat - **Layout:** Stéphanie Benoit - **Translation:** Lyall Pratt - **Proofreading:** Matt Gay, Eleni Salemi - **Edition:** Clémence Mathé